Motorcycle Road & Racing Chassis

A modern review of the best independents

Keith Noakes • Foreword by Mick Grant

Bakker • Bimota • Dresda • Egli • Harris • Hejira • Magni • Maxton
P&M • PDQ • Quasar • Rickman • Segale • Seeley • Spondon

Also from Veloce Publishing –

SpeedPro Series
4-Cylinder Engine – How to Blueprint & Build a Short Block for High Performance (Hammill)
Alfa Romeo DOHC High-Performance Manual (Kartalamakis)
Alfa Romeo V6 Engine High-Perfomance Manual (Kartalamakis)
BMC 998cc A-Series Engine – How to Power Tune (Hammill)
1275cc A-Series High-Performance Manual (Hammill)
Camshafts – How to Choose & Time them for Maximum Power (Hammill)
Cylinder Heads – How to Build, Modify & Power Tune Updated & Revised Edition (Burgess & Gollan)
Distributor-type Ignition Systems – How to Build & Power Tune (Hammill)
Fast Road Car – How to Plan and Build Revised & Updated Colour New Edition (Stapleton)
Ford SOHC 'Pinto' & Sierra Cosworth DOHC Engines – How to Power Tune Updated & Enlarged Edition (Hammill)
Ford V8 – How to Power Tune Small Block Engines (Hammill)
Harley-Davidson Evolution Engines – How to Build & Power Tune (Hammill)
Holley Carburetors – How to Build & Power Tune Revised & Updated Edition (Hammill)
Jaguar XK Engines – How to Power Tune Revised & Updated Colour Edition (Hammill)
MG Midget & Austin-Healey Sprite – How to Power Tune Updated & Revised Edition (Stapleton)
MGB 4-Cylinder Engine – How to Power Tune (Burgess)
MGB V8 Power – How to Give Your, Third Colour Edition (Williams)
MGB, MGC & MGB V8 – How to Improve (Williams)
Mini Engines – How to Power Tune on a Small Budget Colour Edition (Hammill)
Motorcycle-engined Racing Car – How to Build (Pashley)
Motorsport – Getting Started (Collins)
Motorsports Datalogging (Templeman)
Nitrous Oxide High-Performance Manual (Langfield)
Rover V8 Engines – How to Power Tune (Hammill)
Sportscar/Kitcar Suspension & Brakes – How to Build & Modify Enlarged & Updated 2nd Edition (Hammill)
SU Carburettor High-Performance Manual (Hammill)
Supercar, How to Build (Thompson)
Suzuki 4x4 – How to Modify for Serious Off-Road Action (Richardson)
Tiger Avon Sportscar – How to Build Your Own Updated & Revised 2nd Edition (Dudley)
TR2, 3 & TR4 – How to Improve (Williams)
TR5, 250 & TR6 – How to Improve (Williams)
TR7 & TR8, How to Improve (Williams)
V8 Engine – How to Build a Short Block for High Performance (Hammill)
Volkswagen Beetle Suspension, Brakes & Chassis – How to Modify for High Performance (Hale)
Volkswagen Bus Suspension, Brakes & Chassis – How to Modify for High Performance (Hale)
Weber DCOE, & Dellorto DHLA Carburetors – How to Build & Power Tune 3rd Edition (Hammill)

Those were the days ... Series
Alpine Trials & Rallies 1910-1973 (Pfundner)
Austerity Motoring (Bobbitt)
Brighton National Speed Trials (Gardiner)
British Police Cars (Walker)
British Woodies (Peck)
Crystal Palace by (Collins)
Dune Buggy Phenomenon (Hale)
Dune Buggy Phenomenon Volume 2 (Hale)
MG's Abingdon Factory (Moylan)
Motor Racing at Brands Hatch in the Seventies (Parker)
Motor Racing at Goodwood in the Sixties (Gardiner)
Motor Racing at Oulton Park in the 1960s (McFadyen)
Motor Racing at Oulton Park in the 1970s (McFadyen)
Short Oval Racing in the 1980s (Neil)
Three Wheelers (Bobbitt)

Enthusiast's Restoration Manual Series
Citroën 2CV, How to Restore (Porter)
Classic Car Bodywork, How to Restore (Thaddeus)
Classic Car Electrics (Thaddeus)
Classic Cars, How to Paint (Thaddeus)
Reliant Regal, How to Restore (Payne)
Triumph TR2/3/3A, How to Restore (Williams)
Triumph TR4/4A, How to Restore (Williams)
Triumph TR5/250 & 6, How to Restore (Williams)
Triumph TR7/8, How to Restore (Williams)
Volkswagen Beetle, How to Restore (Tyler)
VW Bay Window Bus (Paxton)
Yamaha FS1-E, How to Restore (Watts)

Essential Buyer's Guide Series
Alfa GT (Booker)
Alfa Romeo Spider Giulia (Booker)
BMW GS (Henshaw)
BSA Bantam (Henshaw)
BSA Twins (Henshaw)
Citroën 2CV (Paxton)
Citroën ID & DS (Heilig)
Fiat 500 & 600 (Bobbitt)
Jaguar E-type 3.8 & 4.2-litre (Crespin)
Jaguar E-type V12 5.3-litre (Crespin)
Jaguar/Daimler XJ6, XJ12 & Sovereign (Crespin)
Jaguar XJ-S (Crespin)
MGB & MGB GT (Williams)
Mercedes-Benz 280SL-560SL Roadsters (Bass)
Mercedes-Benz 'Pagoda' 230SL, 250SL & 280SL Roadsters & Coupés (Bass)
Morris Minor (Newell)
Porsche 928 (Hemmings)
Rolls-Royce Silver Shadow & Bentley T-Series (Bobbitt)
Subaru Impreza (Hobbs)
Triumph Bonneville (Henshaw)
Triumph TR6 (Williams)
VW Beetle (Cservenka & Copping)
VW Bus (Cservenka & Copping)

Auto-Graphics Series
Fiat-based Abarths (Sparrow)
Jaguar MkI & II Saloons (Sparrow)
Lambretta LI series scooters (Sparrow)

Rally Giants Series
Audi Quattro (Robson)
Big Healey – 100-Six & 3000 (Robson)
Ford Escort MkI (Robson)
Ford Escort RS1800 (Robson)
Lancia Stratos (Robson)
Peugeot 205 T16 (Robson)
Subaru Impreza (Robson)

General
1½-litre GP Racing 1961-1965 (Whitelock)
AC Two-litre Saloons & Buckland Sportscars (Archibald)
According to Carter (Skelton)
Alfa Romeo Giulia Coupé GT & GTA (Tipler)
Alfa Romeo Montreal - The Essential Companion (Taylor)
Alfa Tipo 33 (McDonough & Collins)
Anatomy of the Works Minis (Moylan)
Armstrong-Siddeley (Smith)
Autodrome (Collins & Ireland)
Automotive A-Z, Lane's Dictionary of Automotive Terms (Lane)
Automotive Mascots (Kay & Springate)
Bahamas Speed Weeks, The (O'Neil)
Bentley Continental, Corniche and Azure (Bennett)
Bentley MkVI, Rolls-Royce Silver Wraith, Dawn & Cloud/Bentley R & S-series (Nutland)
BMC Competitions Department Secrets (Turner, Chambers Browning)
BMW 5-Series (Cranswick)
BMW Z-Cars (Taylor)
British 250cc Racing Motorcycles by Chris Pereira
British Cars, The Complete Catalogue of, 1895-1975 (Culshaw & Horrobin)
BRM – a mechanic's tale (Salmon)
BRM V16 (Ludvigsen)
BSA Bantam Bible (Henshaw)
Bugatti Type 40 (Price)
Bugatti 46/50 Updated Edition (Price & Arbey)
Bugatti T44 & T49 (Price & Arbey)
Bugatti 57 2nd Edition (Price)
Caravans, The Illustrated History 1919-1959 (Jenkinson)
Caravans, The Illustrated History from 1960 (Jenkinson)
Carrera Panamericana (Tipler)
Chrysler 300 – America's Most Powerful Car 2nd Edition (Ackerson)
Chrysler PT Cruiser (Ackerson)
Citroën DS (Bobbitt)
Cliff Alison - From the Fells to Ferrari (Gauld)
Cobra – The Real Thing! (Legate)
Cortina – Ford's Bestseller (Robson)
Coventry Climax Racing Engines (Hammill)
Daimler SP250 New Edition (Long)
Datsun Fairlady Roadster to 280ZX – The Z-car Story (Long)
Dino – The V6 Ferrari (Long)
Dodge Charger – Enduring Thunder (Ackerson)
Dodge Dynamite! (Grist)
Draw & Paint Cars – How to (Gardiner)
Drive on the Wild Side, A – 20 extreme driving adventures from around the world (Weaver)
Ducati 750 Bible, The (Falloon)
Ducati 860, 900 and Mille Bible, The (Falloon)
Dune Buggy, Building a – The Essential Manual (Shakespeare)
Dune Buggy Files (Hale)
Dune Buggy Handbook (Hale)
Edward Turner: the man behind the motorcycles (Clew)
Fiat & Abarth 124 Spider & Coupé (Tipler)
Fiat & Abarth 500 & 600 2nd edition (Bobbitt)
Fiats, Great Small (Ward)
Fine Art of the Motorcycle Engine, The (Peirce)
Ford F100/F150 Pick-up 1948-1996 (Ackerson)
Ford F150 1997-2005 (Ackerson)
Ford GT – Then, and Now (Streather)
Ford GT40 (Legate)
Ford in Miniature (Olson)
Ford Model Y (Roberts)
Ford Thunderbird from 1954, The Book of the (Long)
Forza Minardi! (Vigar)
Funky Mopeds (Skelton)
Funky Motorcycles (Skelton)
Gentleman Jack (Gauld)
GM in Miniature (Olson)
GT – The World's Best GT Cars 1953-73 (Dawson)
Hillclimbing & sprinting – The essential manual (Short)
Honda NSX (Long)
Jaguar, The Rise of (Price)
Jaguar XJ-S (Long)
Jeep CJ (Ackerson)
Jeep Wrangler (Ackerson)
Karmann-Ghia Coupé & Convertible (Bobbitt)
Lambretta Bible, The (Davies)
Lancia 037 (Collins)
Lancia Delta HF Integrale (Blaettel & Wagner)
Land Rover, The Half-Ton Military (Cook)
Laverda Twins & Triples Bible 1968-1986 (Falloon)
Lea-Francis Story, The (Price)
Lexus Story, The (Long)
little book of smart, The (Jackson)
Lola – The Illustrated History (1957-1977) (Starkey)
Lola – All the Sports Racing & Single-Seater Racing Cars 1978-1997 (Starkey)
Lola T70 – The Racing History & Individual Chassis Record 3rd Edition (Starkey)
Lotus 49 (Oliver)
MarketingMobiles, The Wonderful Wacky World of (Hale)
Mazda MX-5/Miata 1.6 Enthusiast's Workshop Manual (Grainger & Shoemark)
Mazda MX-5/Miata 1.8 Enthusiast's Workshop Manual (Grainger & Shoemark)
Mazda MX-5 Miata: the book of the world's favourite sportscar (Long)
Mazda MX-5 Miata Roadster (Long)
MGA (Price Williams)
MGB & MGB GT – Expert Guide (Auto-Doc Series) (Williams)
MGB Electrical Systems (Astley)
Micro Caravans (Jenkinson)
Micro Trucks (Mort)
Microcars at large! (Quellin)
Mini Cooper – The Real Thing! (Tipler)
Mitsubishi Lancer Evo, the road car & WRC story (Long)
Montlhéry, the story of the Paris autodrome (Boddy)
Morgan Maverick (Lawrence)
Morris Minor, 60 years on the road (Newell)
Moto Guzzi Sport & Le Mans Bible (Falloon)
Motor Movies – The Posters! (Veysey)
Motor Racing – Reflections of a Lost Era (Carter)
Motorcycle Road & Racing Chassis Designs (Knoakes)
Motorhomes, The Illustrated History (Jenkinson)
Motorsport in colour, 1950s (Wainwright)
Nissan 300ZX & 350Z – The Z-Car Story (Long)
Pass the Theory and Practical Driving Tests (Gibson & Hoole)
Peking to Paris 2007 (Young)
Plastic Toy Cars of the 1950s & 1960s (Ralston)
Pontiac Firebird (Cranswick)
Porsche Boxster (Long)
Porsche 356 (2nd edition) (Long)
Porsche 911 Carrera – The Last of the Evolution (Corlett)
Porsche 911R, RS & RSR, 4th Edition (Starkey)
Porsche 911 – The Definitive History 1963-1971 (Long)
Porsche 911 – The Definitive History 1971-1977 (Long)
Porsche 911 – The Definitive History 1977-1987 (Long)
Porsche 911 – The Definitive History 1987-1997 (Long)
Porsche 911 – The Definitive History 1997-2004 (Long)
Porsche 911SC 'Super Carrera' – The Essential Companion (Streather)
Porsche 914 & 914-6: The Definitive History Of The Road & Competition Cars (Long)
Porsche 924 (Long)
Porsche 944 (Long)
Porsche 993 'King of Porsche' – The Essential Companion (Streather)
Porsche 996 'Supreme Porsche' – The Essential Companion (Streather)
Porsche Racing Cars – 1953 to 1975 (Long)
Porsche Racing Cars – 1976 on (Long)
Porsche – The Rally Story (Meredith)
Porsche: Three Generations of Genius (Meredith)
RAC Rally Action! (Gardiner)
Rallye Sport Fords: the inside story (Moreton)
Redman, Jim – 6 Times World Motorcycle Champion: The Autobiography (Redman)
Rolls-Royce Silver Shadow/Bentley T Series Corniche & Camargue Revised & Enlarged Edition (Bobbitt)
Rolls-Royce Silver Spirit, Silver Spur & Bentley Mulsanne 2nd Edition (Bobbitt)
RX-7 – Mazda's Rotary Engine Sportscar (updated & revised new edition) (Long)
Scooters & Microcars, The A-Z of popular (Dan)
Scooter Lifestyle (Grainger)
Singer Story: Cars, Commercial Vehicles, Bicycles & Motorcycles (Atkinson)
SM – Citroën's Maserati-engined Supercar (Long & Claverol)
Subaru Impreza: the road car and WRC story (Long)
Taxi! The Story of the 'London' Taxicab (Bobbitt)
Tinplate Toy Cars of the 1950s & 1960s (Ralston)
Toyota Celica & Supra, The book of Toyota's Sports Coupés (Long)
Toyota MR2 Coupés & Spyders (Long)
Triumph Motorcycles & the Meriden Factory (Hancox)
Triumph Speed Twin & Thunderbird Bible (Woolridge)
Triumph Tiger Cub Bible (Estall)
Triumph Trophy Bible (Woolridge)
Triumph TR6 (Kimberley)
Unraced (Collins)
Velocette Motorcycles – MSS to Thruxton Updated & Revised (Burris)
Virgil Exner – Visioneer: The official biography of Virgil M Exner designer extraordinaire (Grist)
Volkswagen Bus Book, The (Bobbitt)
Volkswagen Bus or Van to Camper, How to Convert (Porter)
Volkswagens of the World (Glen)
VW Beetle Cabriolet (Bobbitt)
VW Beetle – The Car of the 20th Century (Copping)
VW Bus – 40 years of Splitties, Bays & Wedges (Copping)
VW Bus Book, The (Bobbitt)
VW Golf: five generations of fun (Copping & Cservenka)
VW – The air-cooled era (Copping)
VW T5 Camper Conversion Manual (Porter)
VW Campers (Copping)
Works Minis, The Last (Purves & Brenchley)
Works Rally Mechanic (Moylan)

First published in November 2007 by Veloce Publishing Limited, 33 Trinity Street, Dorchester DT1 1TT, England. Fax 01305 268864/e-mail info@veloce.co.uk/web www.veloce.co.uk or www.velocebooks.com.
ISBN: 978-1-845841-30-0/UPC: 6-36847-04130-4

Readers with ideas for automotive books, or books on other transport or related hobby subjects, are invited to write to the editorial director of Veloce Publishing at the above address.
British Library Cataloguing in Publication Data - A catalogue record for this book is available from the British Library. Typesetting, design and page make-up all by Veloce Publishing Ltd on Apple Mac.
Printed in India by Replika Press.

Motorcycle
Road & Racing
Chassis

A modern review of the best independents

VELOCE PUBLISHING
THE PUBLISHER OF FINE AUTOMOTIVE BOOKS

Keith Noakes • Foreword by Mick Grant

akker • Bimota • Dresda • Egli • Harris • Hejira • Magni • Maxton
P&M • PDQ • Quasar • Rickman • Segale • Seeley • Spondon

Contents

Foreword 5

Acknowledgements 6

Introduction 7

    A unique contribution.. 8

1 Nico Bakker 9
2 Bimota 23
    Bimota: 1973 to date 26
    Gucci, Ferrari ... Bimota 31
3 Dresda Autos 32
    Design and ride 41
4 Egli Motorradtechnik AG 45
    The Enfield connection 46
    Backbone of steel 48
5 Harris Performance Products 49
    Teamwork 64
6 Hejira Racing HRD 72
7 Magni 81
    Power and style 88
8 Maxton Engineering 91
9 P & M Motorcycles 101
    Go it alone?.. 112
10 PDQ 113
    Move to suspension 116
11 Quasar.. 117
12 Rickman 120
    Distinguished service.. 129
13 Colin Seeley Racing 130
    Original replicas 142
14 Segale 145
15 Spondon Engineering.. 154
16 Overview 169

Index 173

Foreword

From the beginning of motorcycle sport, riders have striven to improve performance, and the rider is surely the best judge of what is required to do that. Of course, in many cases, lack of power is the problem, but often there is ample power which cannot be used to the full because of poor handling.

To overcome these handling problems many riders carried out modifications to the frame or chassis and, in some cases, built completely new frames. In the early post-war years, when the motorcycle factories were only just getting back into operation, development programmes to produce competition motorcycles were rare, so more and more home-built frames began to appear. Some of these were so successful that the riders or builders began to make frames for those who didn't have the ability to do it themselves. Thus, the business of independent frame maker was born.

As the larger well-known factories began to produce more over-the-counter racing motorcycles, competition grew fiercer and the quest for better performance intensified. This trend gathered pace with the Japanese factories, which have always used success in competition to enhance their road bike sales – they soon began to produce over-the-counter competition machinery as well as running their own factory race teams.

Of course, club racers still had to do things their own way. I well remember a race meeting at Brands Hatch in 1974: after practice we had a fairly serious steering problem with the air-cooled KR750 Kawasaki, and not having access to a multitude of setting parts, as is the modern trend, the only way was to hacksaw the headstock out, reposition it, and bronze weld it back in. I finished the job at 2am. Luckily for me, I concentrated on the riding and not on chassis development, as the result on this occasion did not warrant the midnight oil burnt!

In many cases, Japanese engine development was ahead of chassis design and, before long, some of these engines were being housed in independently made frames. This process accelerated when some Japanese factory racers began to use frames built by some of the, by now well known, independent frame makers, who by this stage were the experts. These independents extended their business by the production of road machines and, in fact, many independent frame making companies throughout the world now produce a wide range of exotic road bikes as their main business.

There is no doubt that the independent frame makers have made a major contribution to the development of motorcycle frames or chassis. This book sets out to tell the story of the people and the companies that have, and are still, making a significant contribution to motorcycle frame design.

Mick Grant

Mick Grant in action.

Acknowledgements

I would like to thank the persons and companies listed here for their invaluable help during the writing of this book.

Bimota • Steve and Lester Harris • Bob Stevenson of Spondon Engineering • Colin Seeley • Dave Degens of Dresda Autos • Nico Bakker • Fritz Egli • Richard Peckett of P&M Motorcycles • Ron Williams of Maxton • Segali Corsa • Derek Chittenden of Hejira • Larry Webb of PDQ Developments • Malcolm Newell of Quasar • Derek and Don Rickman • Ken Sprayson • Magni

Plus a special thanks to Roy Jackson, my very patient, and long-suffering, typist. Thanks also to Roland Brown, Oli Tennent, Phil Masters, Graeme Bell and EMAP for additional photographs, and Golden Goose for the Harris Sauber photograph.

Introduction

Since World War II, many clever engineers and enthusiasts – and some not so clever – have built motorcycle frames, whether for road or competition, the latter including trials, motocross, record breaking and, of course, road racing. Some were built with little thought for their design, so success was not always forthcoming.

All these frames were built for one or two main reasons. First of all, in the early post-war years, the urge to go racing or compete in some form of motorcycle event was often frustrated because suitable machinery was not available, or because what was available was outdated. Secondly, as has always been the case, competition gave a strong incentive to gain some technical advantage which, hopefully, would lead to a performance edge on the track.

Many very clever designers surfaced during this period, but often excellent frames evolved from a combination of engineering skills and an intimate knowledge of what was required. This resulted in modification of existing machinery until the desired design performance was achieved.

Apart from the many fine one-off or limited production frames to emerge during this period, in many cases the builders' natural

Ken Sprayson; his knowledge and welding skills were instrumental in helping many budding motorcycle frame makers turn their ideas into reality.

engineering skill resulted in fully-fledged commercial businesses: the independent frame makers described in this book.

Some of those covered no longer trade, but are included because of their contribution to the progress of the independent frame-making business. However, this is also the record of some of those who have been successful, and those who are still designing and building exciting motorcycles using engines from mainstream manufacturers, housed in their own frames.

A unique contribution

No book on motorcycle frame making could be written without mention of Ken Sprayson, or rather, Reynolds, the tubing manufacturer, and Ken Sprayson. Reynolds had been a major source of the steel tubing utilized in the manufacture of motorcycle frames from the early 1900s, but in the immediate post-war years it also undertook the design and production of frames. In addition to supplying the steel tubing, Reynolds was also expert in the use of the material. This expertise was passed on to many new frame makers in the United Kingdom and overseas via Ken Sprayson.

During World War II, Reynolds Tube Co had gained much experience in the manufacture and use of its high quality steel tubing in the aircraft industry. After the war the company began to look for alternative outlets for its expertise, due to the obvious decline in aircraft requirements. During the early 1950s, this expertise found a place in the manufacture of welded motorcycle frames. With its expert knowledge of bending and welding steel tubing, Reynolds often built pre-production frames for the major motorcycle manufacturers.

The first, and very significant, frame contract undertaken by Reynolds was the, now-famous, Norton Featherbed frame. All Featherbeds were made by Reynolds after Rex McCandless made the first six in 1950. After the Featherbed, Reynolds made Norton Commando frames before NVT had them made in Italy.

Even then, Reynolds was involved in rectifying the Italian-made frames.

Other firms to take advantage of the tubing maker's expertise were BSA and Ariel, for whom Reynolds built trials frames. In the boom years of the 1950s, Reynolds also built welded frames for many of the post-war motorcycle manufacturers, including Ambassador, Excelsior, Dayton, Douglas, DKW, Tandon, Velocette, AJS, Vernon, DKR and Royal Enfield. Some were in the early stages of setting themselves up to become the independent frame makers described in this book. Among them were Seeley and Rickman, two of the earliest independents.

Reynolds continued to offer its excellent service until the early 1980s. Throughout this period of the company's history, Ken Sprayson was its expert in the use of specialized steel tubes. He passed on his welding skills to many, some of whom became well-known frame makers in their own right. To this day, many declare that Ken Sprayson played an important part in their beginnings.

Ken may have been the welding expert to whom many turned for guidance, but this was only one of his skills. He was also responsible for the design and construction of many specials; that is, competition frames to suit a range of engines for a variety of formulae. During the 1950s, many famous riders were to take advantage of Ken Sprayson's skills, among them Jeff Smith, Geoff Duke, Mike Hailwood and John Surtees.

Although Reynolds closed its welded assembly business in 1981, Ken Sprayson maintained his involvement with motorcycle design and manufacture, and this included spending a few years with BSA. Today, many of the great independent motorcycle frame makers acknowledge their debt to him for the time in the early post-war years when he imparted his talents to many as a new, growing industry was getting under way.

Keith Noakes

one

Nico Bakker

By the early 1970s, Nico Bakker, a very accomplished motorcycle road racer, had reached a point in his career where his ultimate performance was being restricted by the machinery he was riding. However, this was not due, as in many cases, to a lack of power or reliability – Nico had the right engines, and his racing performance demonstrated his riding ability. The problem lay in the handling of his bike, and this is the point where the Nico Bakker story really starts. As a purely private venture, he decided to build a racing motorcycle frame for his own use.

This first Bakker frame was built to very high standards, using only the very best materials. This high quality was to become a Nico Bakker trademark, and has led to a lasting reputation for excellence of finish. That first frame also proved to be the starting point for a new business, as the very marked

improvement in Nico Bakker's race results with this home-built frame was noted by the motorcycle racing fraternity. It wasn't very long before requests from other private owners for purpose-built frames began to reach Nico. His first commercial frame was for

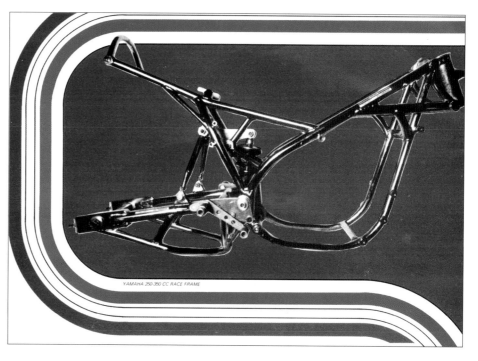

YAMAHA 250-350 CC RACE FRAME

A 1982 Bakker race frame, built to house Yamaha 250 and 350cc engines.

Motorcycle Road & Racing Chassis

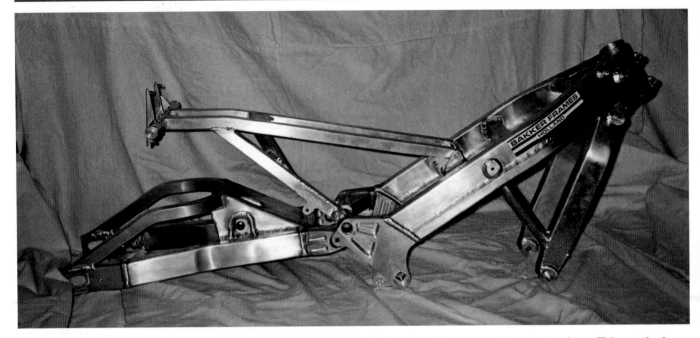

A typical Nico Bakker frame, complete with rear swingarm. It is fabricated from aluminium extrusions. This particular example is a 125cc race frame, of the type used by Peter Ottl.

someone else who was to become famous in motorcycle racing. In 1974, fellow Dutchman Wil Hartog asked Nico to build a frame to house a 250cc Yamaha engine.

At the beginning of his frame-building career, Nico constructed his frames from steel tubing in the traditional manner, but his racing experience gave him the knowledge of exactly where to put the various tubes to achieve the optimum performance from the frame he was building. This quality of design was matched by the use of the best materials, and demand for Bakker frames was strong.

By the mid to late 1970s, Nico Bakker was producing frames for a wide range of engines, from 50 to 1000cc, and in many diferent forms. In fact, his versatility was such that almost any engine was eligible for the Nico Bakker treatment, and his list of customers was growing continually. It included some very well-known top-class riders such as Phil Read, Cecotto, Agostini, Kork Ballington, Jack Middelburg and many others. The comparatively short time in which this demand was achieved is an indication of the admiration that Bakker machines commanded from the motorcycle racing fraternity.

Amongst the frames designed and built during this period was one to house a 125cc Morbidelli engine. Like many others produced by Nico Bakker, this frame could be purchased as a kit into which all the original parts would fit, enabling the customer to rebuild his own machine into the high-performance frame.

Another engine catered for was the Suzuki 1000cc four, the frame offered in road or race trim. The main difference was that the race version utilized a monoshock suspension system, as did the little Morbidelli frame. The 1000 frame was also available in versions to accept the other four-cylinder Japanese motors of the time: Honda 750 and 950cc; Kawasaki 900 and 1000; Suzuki 750 and 1100.

Also popular and successful during this period was a frame for the famous Yamaha TZ. When supplied as a kit, the frame would accommodate all original 250 or 350 parts. In addition, all the other parts, such as petrol tanks, fully-tuned exhaust systems, fairings, seats and wheels were – and still are – produced by Nico Bakker to his usual high standard.

This line of frame design – that is the high quality, tubular steel type – continued into the 1980s, and where the engines remained popular or competitive, Nico continued to supply the relevant frames. For example, the TZ frame was still being produced, but in typical Bakker fashion, it included detail modifications in an effort to optimize the performance. It would still accept the 250 or 350cc TZ engine, and it could be purchased as a complete machine or in kit form. The 1000 frame was also still available to house a range of engines, and examples such as the Suzuki 1000 and the Kawasaki 1000 or 1100-engined machines were offered in race or street-legal forms.

Another popular model from the Bakker works at this time

was a street-legal frame for the six-cylinder Honda CBX. Other frames to come from this prolific builder included race frames for the Cagiva 500 and Rotax 250 engines. The latter incorporated an interesting feature for this period: not only was the rear suspension monoshock, but the shock itself was mounted horizontally, under the crankcase. Such innovation was indicative of Nico Bakker's continual striving for technical improvement.

That was underlined during the mid to late 1980s, when he began to use aluminium in his frame designs, including swingarms. Both frames and swingarm utilized pre-formed aluminium extrusions and tubes. Considerable modification of the extrusion was often required, along with varying amounts of aluminium fabrication to achieve the required result. This would depend on the style or design of the frame or swingarm. The use of extrusions was ideally suited to the construction of the widely-used, twin-spar type frame, which was – and still is – a very popular frame style suitable for many engine configurations.

Nico took to the use of aluminium as a frame material in the same professional manner that he did with steel tubing. He chose the very best quality materials, and aimed for a very high standard of construction and finish. During the latter half of the 1980s, the fabricated aluminium frame became the standard method of construction in the Bakker factory.

From the very beginning, Nico Bakker has always been prepared to design and build one-off or short-run examples of his frames to house almost any type or make of engine. However, he has always had a range of catalogued models that have become popular and, therefore, created a demand. This range of standard frames includes both race and road examples. In most cases, these can be supplied as finished machines or as frame kits.

In the early 1990s, the Bakker range included a full-race spec aluminium twin-spar frame and swingarm to house 125cc engines. In contrast is the Special Formula 1 design, a fabricated twin-spar frame that could be supplied with, or to house, engines from Suzuki, Kawasaki, Honda and Yamaha, in capacities from 750 to 1100cc. In effect, this was a whole range of machines in one design, but this particular frame had something that rendered it extra special: it supported a single-leg rear suspension in place of a conventional swingarm.

The single-leg was of Nico Bakker design and manufacture, and was fabricated from aluminium extrusions, and it remains unique. The single-leg could also be bought as a complete unit – leg, damper, brake, wheel and mudguard – to fit most frames from 250 to 1100cc.

Unlike Bakker's sports and racing machines, the BMW Kangaroo was quite different, a big traillie based on the BMW R100GS, and offered as a complete bike. The air-cooled flat-twin engine and shaft drive were housed in a fabricated, aluminium twin-spar frame, welded to swingarm pivot mounts that were machined from solid. Square-section alloy tubes ran under the engine in normal cradle fashion, while the rear suspension was designed to accommodate the standard shaft-drive unit.

Upside down White Power forks took care of the front suspension, with stopping handled by two Brembo 300mm floating discs and four-piston calipers at the front, and the standard BMW disc of the rear. Running on 17in wheels, all this made the Kangaroo an incredible street-legal machine, wrapped up in very distinctive and stylish aluminium body panels, or fibreglass panels for those wishing to save some of the cost.

An independent professional rider reported the BMW-based Bakker as being an excellent handling road machine, with good torque from the flat-twin and a claimed top speed of 125mph. The first ten Kangaroos were snapped up quickly, resulting in Bakker putting a much larger batch into production.

In fact, BMW engine lovers were well catered for by Nico Bakker, as he also offered a bike based around the K100 liquid-cooled four-cylinder engine. This too used a fabricated aluminium twin-spar frame with USD White Power front forks, plus Brembo four-piston caliper in a 16in front wheel, and an 18in wheel at the rear. The complete machine weighed in at 188kg, which was only 3kg heavier than the Kangaroo, due to the larger, liquid-cooled engine. The Nico Bakker BMW K100 Special, as it was designated, was finished off with stylish GRP bodywork and had a claimed top speed of 240mph. It was an interesting alternative take on BMW's 'Brick' offering a K-powered sports bike long before BMW itself did.

From the very beginning, Nico Bakker has been extremely versatile and has pioneered a wide range of technical advances, but one masterpiece crowned all of these achievements. The QCS (Quick Change System) was a unique machine in that both wheels were single-side mounted and easy to change (hence the name) with both hub-centre steering and the Bakker single-leg rear suspension.

But of course, the QCS wasn't designed that way simply to improve wheel changing times. The use of hub-centre steering resulted in constant steering geometry and wheelbase measurement. These two major benefits can never be achieved with even the best conventional front fork layout. The QCS layout also allowed quicker and easier suspension adjustments, a major advantage for road-race machines.

Although hub-centre steering is not new, Nico Bakker designed his version to take full advantage of the technical possibilities it offers. This remarkable design utilized axial pivot steering, which means that the kingpin (formerly the front fork) angle remains constant during suspension movement, resulting

The BMW-based Kangaroo, using the R100GS air-cooled boxer engine, along with the BMW gearbox and shaft-drive.

This aluminium twin-spar frame houses a BMW K100 engine. The four-cylinder, water-cooled powerplant retains the factory gearbox and shaft drive. It is designated the K100 Special.

This aluminium twin-spar Formula 1 frame will accept a range of engines, including Suzuki, Kawasaki, Honda and Yamaha, with capacities ranging from 750 to 1100cc. Note the use of the standard Nico Bakker single-leg rear suspension.

in little or no trail change, and the result was a machine with more neutral handling than a conventional system could deliver.

Due to Bakker's own six-piston brake caliper, braking equal to a twin-disc set-up was achieved using a single ventilated disc, which brought a weight saving, but more importantly, the central position of the single disc in the front wheel meant that its gyrocopic effect had a less negative influence on roadholding. The single central disc also had a unique cooling system, air being forced through a cleverly-designed hollow front mudguard onto the disc, which itself was ventilated. The rear brake used a twin-piston Brembo caliper.

All this sounds like a very formidable package to be ridden by experts only, but such was not the case. In fact, the QCS was claimed to be much simpler to ride than motorcycles of conventional layout. Road test reports by professional riders described it as being a joy to ride, in terms of comfort and outright handling. They remarked on the high degree of road feel, something reported as lacking in other hub-centre steering

designs, while another notable point was the lack of road shock felt through the handlebars. As there were no forks for mounting the clip-on bars, Nico fitted a machined alloy plate on a short headstock running on roller bearings. Attaching the clip-ons to this gave the overall appearance of normal handlebars.

The positive feel and lack of road shock were due to the unique front suspension and steering arrangement. The front suspension was connected to a front subframe at the mounting points, which meant that the forces were not concentrated at one point, as is the case with the steering head of conventional front forks. Another advantage of this system was that none of the suspension movement was transmitted to the handlebars. All this improved rider comfort which, in turn, reduced fatigue, something of prime importance to long-distance road riders and endurance racers. The QCS was enclosed by beautiful bodywork, optimised for aerodynamics and comfort, and designed by Cees Smit, and of course was finished to the same very high standard as the rest of Bakker's products.

Another Nico Bakker first: a six-piston front brake caliper, shown fitted to a QCS.

The exciting QCS, minus its bodywork. Note the hub-centre steering and single-leg rear suspension. The engine is used as a stressed member of the frame, the front and rear subframes being bolted directly to it.

A QCS finished in road trim. This one is based on a Honda 750cc engine.

Another road-going QCS, but this time with a Yamaha engine.

Nico Bakker's exciting BMW-based Bomber, which makes use of components from the R1100RS.

The prototype QCS was built around a Honda RVF750, but the production road version used Yamaha FZR1000 parts. It's significant that the complete QCS actually weighed approximately 10 per cent less than the original Yamaha. There was actually a complete range of QCS bikes, to accept 250 and 500cc race engines as well as 750 and 1000cc four-strokes.

It's clear that Bakker had a good relationship with BMW, and he actually acted as consultant when the Bavarian campany was developing its Telelever front suspension. So the Kangaroo and K1100 weren't Bakker's only BMW-based bikes. The Bomber was a high performance road-going sports machine based around BMW's eight-valve 1100cc oil-cooled flat-twin. This used the engine as a fully-stressed member, the front end of the frame consisting of an alloy box-section bolted directly to the engine and carrying the suspension. The rear suspension was a single-sided swingarm that enclosed the driveshaft.

Bakker's version of telelever front suspension was based on a single pivoting wishbone, which operated a suspension unit mounted behind the steering head. This

The single-leg rear suspension unit. It comes complete with wheel, transmission damper, brake and mudguard.

Motorcycle Road & Racing Chassis

What Bakker did to the Harley-Davidson, in 1994. (Courtesy Roland Brown)

type of suspension is claimed to maintain a higher degree of steering geometry under braking and cornering than conventional forks, and Nico has designed the front suspension to give a ride height that enhanced the handling necessary on a sports bike of this calibre, while maintaining the overall appearance of conventional forks.

As with the front end, the rear alloy tubular subframe was bolted directly to the engine and gearbox unit. It carried a carbon fibre seat, while the gearbox, brakes (ABS is an option), instruments, electronics, exhaust and lights were all standard R1100RS items. Fuel was carried in a Bakker 22 litre alloy tank, which was beautifully styled, along with the rest of the Bakker bodywork. This elegant and modern design weighed in dry at

Opposite top: A version of the Kangaroo, based on the older version of the BMW Boxer engine.

202kg, and was a true sports bike, with an estimated top speed of 138mph.

The range of parts or accessories continues to grow along with the range of complete machines. The Bakker factory will still produce anything from the earlier years if required: the Kangaroo for example based on the old air-cooled BMW flat-twin. The Bomber is still part of the range too, to suit BMW's eight-valve

Right: The beautiful-looking Grizzly, built to house almost any four-cylinder engine.

Motorcycle Road & Racing Chassis

twin, and the Barracuda is a complete motorcycle designed to accept big V-twins, such as the Suzuki TL1000, Honda VTR or Ducati. The well-known Grizzly can be supplied with any four-cylinder engine, including the Suzuki GSX-R and Honda CBR. Then there's the supermono racer, which will take Rotax, Yamaha, Honda or any other big single-cylinder engine. The Hawk is based on Honda's Hawk, the 650cc engine expanded to 700cc and tuned to produce twice the horsepower.

Over the years, the Bakker works has produced many one-off or small production runs of machines for special needs, a prime example of this being an off-road or enduro machine built around the BMW GS flat-twin. It weighs 30kg less than BMW's factory bike.

The diversity of Bakker's range and the innovation behind his work is clear – not only that, but he has put these advanced machines into production, and maybe that is the true achievement.

This Bakker machine is designed around the Honda CBX 1000 six-cylinder engine.

Nico Bakker

The bike shown here could be built to house Rotax, Yamaha, Honda or any large single-cylinder engine designed for Supermono racing.

The Barracuda is a Bakker design intended for larger V-twins such as the Suzuki TL1000. the Honda VTR and the Ducati.

The Bakker Enduro machine utilising the BMW Boxer engine. This machine is an amazing 30kg lighter than the standard bike.

This exciting Bakker machine is the Hawk, designed and built round the Honda 650cc engine, but modified to 700cc and tuned to give twice the power of the standard machine.

Motorcycle Road & Racing Chassis

A typical tubular frame by Bakker. Tubular frames can be built in aluminium or steel tubing depending on requirements.

This photograph shows a modern fabricated aluminium chassis or frame. The renowned Bakker quality can be seen in this example.

two

Bimota

For many years, Bimota has maintained a reputation for designing and building exciting motorcycles with excellent styling, superb finish, and ever-advancing technical design. But unlike most independent motorcycle frame makers, Bimota was not formed to make bikes. In fact, originally the company had no connection with motorcycles at all. Bimota was founded in 1966 by Valerio Bianchi, Guiseppe Morri and Massimo Tamburini. The company name was arrived at by combining the first two letters of each founder member's name. Based in Rimini, it was established to make heating and ventilation ducting. But two of the founders – Morri and Tamburini

– were motorcycle enthusiasts, which is why Bimota became involved in the motorcycle world.

Massimo Tamburini soon began to make use of the company's facilities to work on bikes, and before long, decided to design and build complete chassis. The success of his early

One of the first machines built by Bimota. This 1973 HBI utilized a 750cc four-cylinder Honda engine. The rider is Luigi Anell.

This machine has a frame manufactured completely from steel tubing.

work led to more design and construction, and his obvious talent and abilities were to see a weekend hobby turn into a serious potential business. This potential was eventually exploited to the full when, in 1973, Bimota began to manufacture motorcycles exclusively.

Today, Bimota is a world-famous manufacturer of prestigious and exclusive motorcycles, and has achieved that by sticking to certain principles that were determined from the beginning. These are to produce comparatively small numbers of bikes by hand, using the best possible materials and designs. To maintain its reputation and share of the market, Bimota has strived to lead the field, where possible, with continued innovation, many of its ideas setting the standard for others to follow.

This has been manifest in Bimota's 'no compromise' motorcycles, which aren't designed to satisfy the widest possible market group and so can be tailored for a very specific purpose. Another important principle is that Bimota imposes no budget restrictions on either design or manufacture. The company has a wonderful saying: it designs and builds motorcycles for those people who are prepared to sacrifice everything, in order to sacrifice nothing.

The first Bimota principle is that a motorcycle has to be able to meet the riding requirements of the customer, and not vice versa, which is why Bimotas offer many different adjustments. It also puts great effort into producing very stiff frames, which is why these are as short as practicable – the greater the length, the greater the flex. Materials are also chosen to enhance stiffness.

Another aspect of Bimota quality is that it aims to maintain the closest tolerances possible, achieved by the use of innovative electronic design systems, coupled with the highest possible standards of workmanship. An advanced CAD-CAM system offers very precise design parameters, which are then transferred directly to digitally-controlled manufacturing machines. This

The HB2, again steel tubing wfth an alloy swingarm pivot. This 1981 model has a 900cc Honda engine.

most important test areas for its machines is the race track. Here, technical advances prove their worth, while the all-important reliability is put to the test.

Bimota's bodywork department produces fairings and panels, and also carries out development work on aerodynamics, often in association with other organisations, such as design studios and universities. Quite apart from the advantages of aerodynamic efficiency, this attention to body styling has resulted in Bimota gaining a reputation for avant-garde shapes.

With every effort being made to ensure the ultimate possible quality, the materials used in Bimota's designs are also considered to be the very best for each frame. Where steel tubing is used for a space frame or subframe, only chrome

type of machinery enables a wide variety of components to be machined from solid billet, which combines the lowest possible weight with the highest possible strength.

All this excellence of design and manufacture is supported by Bimota's research and development department, which ensures that the performance and quality of current models is maintained, through experimentation and testing, while advancing development for future models. Even with this excellent research and development department, Bimota claims that one of the

The SB4 with a Suzuki 1100cc engine. Note the use of machined aluminium alloy to link the frame tubes and form the swingarm pivot.

molybdenum tubing is employed. As a large percentage of chassis are now manufactured in alloys, these materials need very special selection. In Bimota's case, it uses some of the expensive alloys to be found in the aerospace industries, such as Anticorodal, Anticorodal 100 and Avional, all of which help optimise the strength-to-weight ratio.

But on its own, using the best materials isn't enough, and the way in which component parts are joined together is of equal importance. To this end, Bimota is a keen advocate of thin welding, which looks neater and is structurally superior to conventional welding. For thin welding to work, the mating faces must fit very accurately prior to welding, as close-fitting components only require a very thin weld to effect a perfect joint. Thin, even welding is less likely to contain blow-holes and other foreign matter, while those close tolerances needed at the joints mean that less stress is built into the frame during the welding process, since the weld does not have to pull the mating parts together and close large gaps. To reduce distortion during welding, Bimota has adopted the single spot-weld method to hold components together initially, after which the weld area

is filled as a secondary operation. Of course, such attention to detail is time consuming and, therefore, much more expensive than mass production methods.

Having made every effort to produce an accurate, top-quality frame, Bimota spares no effort in protecting it. To this end, the steel frames are electrolytically degreased, then finished with a plastic coating. This has great advantages in that it has a very good appearance, while being more flexible than most paints and lacquers, and thus more damage resistant. Aluminium frames and components are anodized to protect their surfaces. The anodized finish becomes part of the surface itself, so is less likely to be porous or crack with any flexing of the frame in use.

There is no production line in the Bimota factory; each bike is assembled by a skilled technician who is responsible for that machine from start to finish. The technician's name is recorded against the frame number, so that if there are any problems or warranty claims on the machine, the company can trace who built it. In any case, every bike is tested thoroughly prior to delivery, including all the electrics, the mechanical components and bodywork.

The Bellaria is based on the standard Bimota aluminium alloy twin-spar frame and running gear, clad with stylish, full bodywork. This model is powered by a Yamaha 600cc engine.

The Biposto, a two-seat version of the popular Dieci.

The high-performance Furano, which features race-style bodywork and the usual aluminium alloy twin-spar frame. Upside-down forks take care of the front suspension and steering, while the engine is a 1000cc Yamaha with integrated ignition and fuel injection.

As well as excellent materials and manufacture, each Bimota frame is highly adjustable. Triple clamps allow adjustment of the front end in every possible direction, which means that height, rake and offset can all be set to their best advantages, and weight distribution optimized. One very useful option on many Bimotas is an adjustable steering head angle, achieved by means of an eccentric system, coupled with unique conical bearings incorporating specially-shaped rollers. Front forks are adjustable for rebound damping and spring preload.

Bimota: 1973 to date

Like so many independently produced motorcycles, Bimotas were race-bred from the very beginning, the first official machine in 1973. This was based on a tubular steel frame and housed a 750cc four-cylinder Honda engine. It also had twin front disc brakes, carried a top-half fairing, and was raced by Luigi Anelli.

For 1974, Bimota used Yamaha engines in the YB1, 350 and 250cc versions being produced. The following year the company turned to Suzuki, with the 500cc SB1, also offering the 500cc Aermacchi AB1. Bimota chose a wider range of engines for 1976, frames being designed and built to house Yamaha 350 and 250cc engines (in the YB2), Aermacchi 250 (AB2), and Morbidelli

250. Larger capacity engines followed in '77, in the form of the SB2, which housed 750cc Suzuki engines, and the KB1, which accepted the Kawasaki four. Bimota made good use of Yamaha 250 and 350 two-strokes in the 1978 YB3, while 1979 was to see the first 1000cc Bimota, the Suzuki-powered SB3.

For 1980, 500cc engines from Kawasaki were used in the KB2 models, while in 1981 Bimota designed and built frames for the Honda 900cc four, the complete bikes designated HB2. By 1982, the larger-capacity engines were in demand again, and to cater for this Bimota built machines to house the Kawasaki 1100, designated KB3.

Big 1100cc units were chosen again for 1983, the SB4 model employing a Suzuki powerplant. That year also saw Bimota take another significant step forward with the introduction of the first Tesi model. This design, designated 2H, was totally new. It dispensed with conventional front forks, instead, using a front swingarm arrangement with hub-centre steering. The rear suspension was also based on a swingarm. Both front and rear systems were damped by a single shock absorber, and this development was to become a very important feature of the Bimota range. The first Tesi model used a 400cc Honda engine.

The half-fairing version of the exciting DB2. The frame is high-quality steel tubing, and the engine a Ducati of 904cc. With a total dry weight of 164kg, the machine has an excellent power-to-weight ratio.

The prototype of Bimota's advanced-technology Tesi. In place of conventional front forks is a swinging arm with hub-centre steering. This model is powered by a 400cc Honda engine.

The later Tesi ID. Powered by a 904cc Ducati V-twin, this stylish machine is an excellent example of Bimota's capabilities.

In 1984, 1100s were popular, and Bimota marketed two of them, the Suzuki-powered SB5 and Honda-engined HB3. Meanwhile, a 750cc version of the Tesi (still Honda sourced) was launched. There was big news in 1985, with the first ever Ducati-powered Bimota, the 750cc DB1, but the company wasn't about to abandon Japanese powerplants, with the Yamaha 750 YB4 and 1200 YB4. These were joined by the 1000cc YB6 in 1987, and the YB4 EXUP the year after that, while the Tesi, too, could now be ordered with a Yamaha 750 engine.

In 1989 the Yamaha 1000cc engine was used in the YB8 model, while the new Bellaria (600cc) and Tuatara (1000cc), both of them Yamaha-engined, were unveiled. Yamaha engines were still in big demand for 1990, and Bimota responded with the YB10, the 1000cc version. Tesi now came with a Ducati option, the 1D 851, while the company also produced a 500cc GP bike.

This is no means a full account of Bimota's output, as it has always produced a range of road and race bikes, but it gives a flavour of what the company was building. More recent bikes included the Dieci, which had an alloy twin-spar type frame, upside down front forks and monoshock rear suspension. The engine was a four-cylinder, 1000cc Yamaha, and the machine was enclosed by a full set of bodywork that encapsulated the fuel tank and the top portion of the alloy frame. The result was

a high-quality, high-performance touring bike in solo form, while a Biposto, or two-seater, version was also catalogued.

The YB8E was more of a sports bike, using the same 1000cc Yamaha mounted in a twin-spar alloy frame, this time with race-style bodywork. Another version of the YB8E, known as the Furano, added fuel injection and uprated ignition. The Bellaria used a similar rolling chassis to the Dieci, but had its own distinctive full bodywork, and wasYamaha 600-powered.

Pride of the fleet for a time was the very exciting Tesi ID 906R. As ever with the Tesi, it had swingarm front suspension with hub-centre steering, now driven by a 904cc, fuel-injected version of Ducati's famous L-twin, with its desmodromic valve gear. The Tesi 1DES, was a special-edition model with distinctive bodywork, produced to celebrate 20 years of Bimota. The 904cc Ducati engine was also used in the DB2, offered in full- and half-fairing versions, both of them lightweight performance bikes with excellent handling.

Most of the Bimota range described here had aluminium alloy frames, although the DB2 frame was of high quality steel tubing. The complete machine weighed in at an amazingly low 164kg for the half-faired version, and 168kg for the fully-faired. By comparison, apart from the Bellaria at 175kg, all the other Bimotas of the time weighed 180kg or more.

1995 Bimoto Supemono, powered by BMW. (Courtesy Phil Masters)

All of these bikes used bought-in engines from major manufacturers, but in 1998 Bimota finally announced a power unit of its own. It was the V-due, a 500cc two-stroke V-twin with a compression ratio of 12:1 and fuel injection. It produced an incredible 105bhp, promising the power of a 750, the weight of a 250, and stunning performance.

But the high-tech two-stroke proved troublesome in practice – the fuel injection system delivered awkward, peaky performance, and eventually all the V-dues were recalled by the factory. There was a plan to convert them all to carburettor operation, and a prototype was built, but by then the company was rapidly running out of money. In 2001 an Italian court declared Bimota bankrupt.

However, the company did revive, and in 2007 was offering a full range of DB5 1000, DB6, SB8K and Tesi 2D. The esteem in which Bimota and its motorcycles are still held is borne out by the active Bimota owners clubs in the UK, Sweden, Norway, Finland and Denmark. It's clear that Bimota has followed an evolutionary path since 1973, making technical and quality advances that have resulted in the well-established company that has the respect of the motorcycling fraternity throughout the world.

Gucci, Ferrari ... Bimota

Bimota established itself as a large, independent manufacturer of advanced motorcycle designs, built to the highest possible standards. Although it has become a prolific builder of road and sport machines, since the company was formed, it has also designed and built many excellent racing bikes. These have proved very competitive, winning 350 races worldwide. Bimota's own factory team has won three World Championships and over 20 Italian Championships, a competition record that any manufacturer would be very proud of. The list of famous riders to race Bimotas is just as impressive, and includes the great Agostini, Read, Lucchinelli, Cecotto, Vucini, Villa, Ekerold, Pileri, Ferrari, Lavado, Mertens and Falappa.

This account illustrates the capability and potential of Bimota, and it is impossible to guess what innovation the company will come up with next.

three

Dresda Autos

Dave Degens received an excellent engineering training in his father's business during the 1950s, and this background was to prove invaluable later. He developed a passion for motorcycles at an early age, and his new-found engineering skills were soon used to carry out modifications, improvements and repairs to a number of machines.

Dave's skills led him to contact Dresda Autos, a retail scooter outlet that took some of his modified machines on a sale-or-return basis. When the owners of Dresda became disenchanted with the shop in 1963, Dave Degens stepped in and bought it. He retained its best scooter mechanic and carried on the retail business, but also added motorcycles to the range.

Although it retained the name, it was inevitable that Dresda's business would change. For as well as being a very competitive racer, Dave Degens had built three Tritons (a marriage of a Triumph engine and a Norton Featherbed frame) and a Norton Rocket prior to buying the shop. There was a ready demand for these high-performance motorcycles and, as a result, Dresda Autos was to become the prolific builder of high-quality, high-performance British twins we know today.

Dave Degens had gained his racing experience by

Dave Degens working on the construction of a Triton in the early days of Dresda Autos, in 1965.

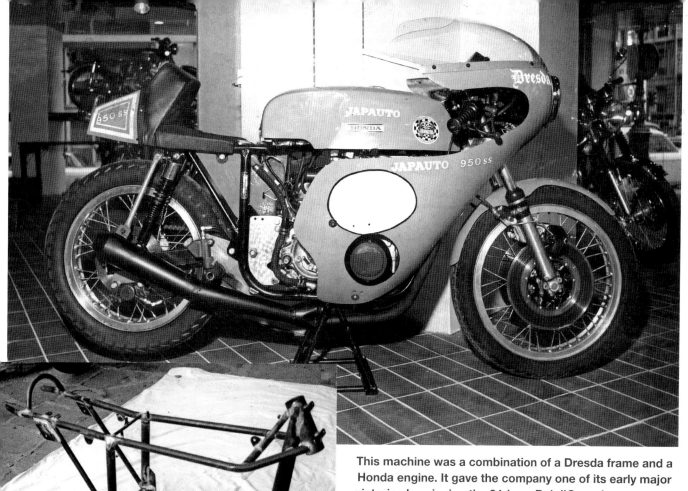

This machine was a combination of a Dresda frame and a Honda engine. It gave the company one of its early major victories by winning the 24-hour Bol d'Or endurance race.

An early Dresda frame just after welding has been completed. This particular frame was made to house a Triumph twin.

successfully competing on such machines as BSA Gold Stars, AJS 7Rs, and of course, Tritons. His racing experience was not always on the larger, more powerful bikes, though, and he is rather proud of a very successful outing on a twin-cylinder Rumi scooter in a race catering for that type of machine.

After buying Dresda Autos, Degens continued to race motorcycles, and, in fact, his riding had not gone unnoticed by others. During the 1964 season, one of the works BMW riders was unable to ride in the 24-hour endurance race in Barcelona, and Dave was offered the ride. This was his introduction to endurance racing, and he proved to have a flair for night riding, doing much of the night riding stint on the BMW.

This fired Dave's enthusiasm for endurance racing, and

he was soon making plans to build a bike and compete in his own right. It was no dream. He engineered a Triumph engine into a Manx Norton Featherbed frame, and used the bike to win the 1965 Barcelona 24-hour race. He later entered a 650cc Triumph-engined bike with a Dresda frame, and with this won at Barcelona again in 1970, the only English rider to have won there on a British bike, and he did it twice!

Dave Degens' ability to produce the best of the Triton hybrids was now well and truly proven, leading to an excellent and exciting line of business. However, although the Triton was good business for Dresda Autos, that didn't stop Dave from pursuing other interesting projects. One such opportunity arose during 1968, when he solved a problem for Yamaha, which was experiencing difficulties with the swingarm of its racers. The problem was a pivot bearing fault, which Dave first identified and then cured by modifying the assembly.

Another Yamaha swingarm problem was to build a new arm to accommodate a new racing tyre, that was too large for the factory swingarm. Dave's replacement was of box-section steel, and some of those who rode Degens-modified Yamahas were Christian Sarron, Rodney Gould and the legendary Barry Sheene.

Another early Dresda machine, utilizing a
Suzuki 500 engine.

A typical frame kit, in this case for a
four-cylinder Honda engine.

Dresda Autos

A model from the early 1980s: the engine is a 750cc K-series Honda.

This machine demonstrates the versatility of Dresda Autos, the frame accommodating a Honda Gold Wing engine. It was built in 1983 for Ken Hull of Honda UK.

Motorcycle Road & Racing Chassis

A short-stroke 350cc Triumph engine in a Dresda race frame.

A 750cc Honda-engined drag bike built by Dresda Autos for Terry Revel. It was a record holder in its class.

This 1977 race bike was built to compete in Spanish national events, the colour scheme being that of the Spanish bank which sponsored the rider. The engine is a 750cc K-series Honda.

In 1969 Dresda Autos produced a chassis to house the Triumph 500cc Daytona engine. The new frame was built from 17swg Reynolds 531 tubing, and, when completed, it weighed in at only 64kg. This lightweight machine made its racing début at Snetterton, ridden by the designer and builder himself, who finished in an exciting second place, by no more than a wheel, after a race-long battle with the works Triumph, ridden by the famous Percy Tait. Two weeks later, Degens used the same bike to win the Scarborough Gold Cup. Both Scarborough and Snetterton were full International meetings, proving that both machine and rider were up to scratch.

During 1970-71, Dresda Autos won a contract to produce a batch of five frames for Christian Vilaseca, to house Honda 750cc engines. The plan was for Dresda to build the complete frames, then Christian Vilaseca would fit the engines. The frames were duly delivered, but soon afterwards an urgent call from Vilaseca suggested that the engines would not fit.

Having built the frames, Degens knew that all was correct, but could not convince the customer of this, so a friendly wager was set. The deal was that he would fly to Paris to fit, or attempt

to fit, an engine. If the engine did go into the frame, Vilaseca would cover the cost of the trip; if it didn't, Dresda would pay for the visit and rectify the faulty frames.

On arrival at the Paris factory, Dave soon spotted why they could not fit the engine. The mechanics were trying to lift it into the frame, but the space between the frame tubes didn't appear large enough. He promptly laid the engine on the workshop floor and then fed the frame over it, passing it over the narrowest part of the engine, then moving it to the correct mounting position. After the drama, these Dresda-frames fared well. One of the Christian Vilaseca machines went on to win the prestigious Bol d'Or 24-hour race, while two more finished in the top six.

The success achieved by Dresda and its products gained the company a high reputation, which resulted in an approach by Yamaha, which wanted a frame to house one of its 750cc

Motorcycle Road & Racing Chassis

A one-off frame for a four-cylinder Kawasaki.

A typical Dresda Triton, comprising a Norton frame and an electric-start Triumph engine. Note the low seat position. This example was built to order for a customer in Japan.

The type of machine for which Dresda is renowned: a Triumph triple in a Norton frame.

Dave Degens in action during 1990. The machine, of course, is a Dresda Triumph.

Man and machine: Dave Degens with his personal Dresda Triumph during 1991. Both saw a full season on the track.

twin-cylinder engines. Dresda was supplied a complete bike, from which the engine was removed and fitted into the Dresda frame. It was during this project that Dave Degens' forward thinking showed itself once more, when he incorporated monoshock rear suspension, quite an advanced feature for the early 1970s.

The Yamaha project would also demonstrate that Dave Degens' skills extended to engines. The Yamaha twin suffered a persistent internal problem; Degens established the cause and carried out modifications to eliminate it. This work led to a contract for Dresda to follow the fault right through, including visiting the Porsche test centre where development on the engine was being carried out. He oversaw the various modifications, and also developed a further mod to rectify a fault that caused the cam chain to destroy its tensioner.

Whilst at the test centre, Dave became aware that an engine under test was not running correctly, and discovered that the throttle slides were fitted incorrectly. Much to everyone's amazement, he corrected the throttle setup, and the engine achieved its expected power output.

With a successful development frame for Yamaha and the engine work, Dave Degens and Dresda Autos had shown their potential to this important manufacturer. Of course, much of the motorcycling public already knew the worth of Dresda's work, having seen that almost any engine would benefit from being fitted into a Dresda frame: Triumph, Norton, BSA, Suzuki, Honda, and Kawasaki units have been used.

In addition to its impressive frames, still being built, Dresda Autos also markets its own swingarm kit, and have always offered a comprehensive modification service. It will modify a frame to take an alternative engine, or convert a dual shock system to monoshock, and carry out other special frame modifcations, such as adding extra tubes to enhance stiffness.

Shown here is a frame being built to house an early JAP 1100cc V-twin. Note the fabricated yokes; the tubes are steel.

More recently, Dave Degens and Dresda Autos have moved to new premises, but continue to utilise their skills and experience to supply the service their race and road customers expect. Although Dresda does not base its business on long run production models, it's kept busy restoring and rebuilding classic machines, many of which are still raced in earnest.

Dresda Autos currently seems to specialise in the manufacture of one-off or small numbers of frames or complete machines to house a wide range of engines. In fact, almost any engine can be catered for, an example being the fitting of a Harley-Davidson engine into a replica Featherbed frame. Another was fitting an early JAP twin into a modern-style frame, resulting in a very rapid bike. Some very exotic projects are undertaken by Dresda, such as the complete rebuild of a 250cc NSU SportMax-engined machine reputed to have been built originally by Reynolds for the legendary Geoff Duke.

Design and ride

Any business that has run from 1963 to the present day and is still thriving has a good track record, but the very competitive environment in which Dresda Autos operates only adds to this considerable achievement. And much of the success is down to Dave Degens himself. Although he has had excellent skilled hands working for him over the years, his own proven skills, coupled with his forward thinking, are without doubt the basis of Dresda's success. He has been involved in many and varied projects, most with great success, though it's interesting that the Dresda Triton is still the company's main line of business.

Perhaps central to all of this is the simple fact that Dave Degens is a very good rider. When the designer can take his latest creation onto the circuit and ride it to its full potential, this has to be a great advantage. For many years, Dresda Autos has produced beautifully-engineered motorcycles, greatly treasured by enthusiasts. If Dave Degens has his way, it will continue to do so.

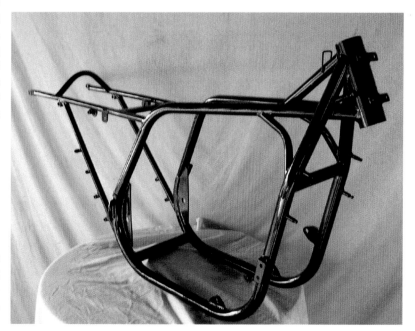

Another Dresda frame, shown in this photograph, is a tubular steel full loop duplex example, built to take a Honda single cam 750cc engine.

four

Egli Motorradtechnik AG

In the field of motorcycle frame design and manufacture, the name Fritz Egli is legendary. Over many years, his reputation for innovation, performance, finish and excellent engineering has become widespread and well established.

Like many other frame makers, Fritz Egli became involved initially by carrying out modifications to improve the performance of existing components, but with his natural talent and flair, it was inevitable that he would move on to greater things.

Fritz Egli raced motorcycles himself, which gave him first-hand knowledge of what was required from a particular frame. This direct experience proved invaluable, in both short- and long-term. Fritz raced a Vincent, but its many handling problems, which on occasion produced alarming speed wobbles, resulted in a difficult machine to

ride. Concerted effort and courage in his riding produced just a single third place over a considerable period.

At this point, Egli made a far-reaching decision: to design

The Egli Red Falcon, which can accommodate Honda or Yamaha single-cylinder engines from 500 to 650cc.

For road or track, the Red Hunter makes use of a four-cylinder Honda engine of up to 1200cc.

and build a new frame for his Vincent, something which would have a major infuence on his life for years to come. The immediate effect of the new frame was very evident, for Fritz Egli won every race he entered in 1968, taking the Swiss Championship. This remarkable improvement in the performance of the Vincent proved two major points: firstly, that the right frame is vital to the ultimate performance of the motorcycle; secondly, that Fritz Egli could both design and build a high performance frame. The die was cast, and many future customers would reap the benefit of his obvious engineering talents.

Egli had actually gone into business during 1965, and since then has proved his versatility by producing an almost endless list of frames for different engines. Moreover, those frames have been built for many different uses, and as well as the beautiful road bikes for which Fritz Egli has become famous, he has produced many competition frames, the majority for road racing, for which he has a special enthusiasm and, of course, first-hand knowledge.

The Vincent frame was followed by frames to house the famous Triumph twin, and later the triple. His first frames for Japanese engines included the Honda 450cc twins and the larger, very popular 750cc four, together with a range of Kawasaki engines, including the H2 and H3. Yamaha two-stroke engines were well used too, most of these for road racing machines with capacities of 250, 350 and 750cc. Laverda, Ducati, BMW and Suzuki engines have all been given the Egli treatment, and even the Harley-Davidson V-twin found its way into an Egli frame.

The utilization of such a wide range of engines illustrates the versatility of Fritz Egli's engineering skills. The range of engines covers not just many different capacities, but widely varying physical size and layout, in frames built for different purposes. Some have been used for drag racing, and he has produced sidecar outfits for a variety of power units, including Suzuki and the Yamaha V-Max. And although there have been many Egli one-offs, he is one of the few independent frame makers to catalogue a range of standard designs.

Motorcycle Road & Racing Chassis

For four-cylinder Kawasaki engines, Egli customers can choose the Bonneville.

In nearly 30 years of production, and these many variants, two significant points stand out in all the Egli frames. One is the persistent use of the rigid backbone layout; almost all Egli frames use a version of this arrangement. The other point is that Fritz Egli has never waivered from the use of steel tubing, and that every frame is fully nickel-plated.

This book is about frame makers, but no account of this type would be complete without mention of Fritz Egli's engine tuning abilities: gas flowing cylinder heads; special cams; reworked crankshafts, valve gear and pistons; and tailored exhaust systems. With these skills at hand, the excellent reputation and performance achievements of Fritz Egli come as no surprise.

Egli's tuning skills were used to good effect on Red Lightning II of 1990, reported at the time as being one of the fastest street-legal production bikes in the world. It used a typical backbone frame, with front forks of Egli design. The Suzuki GSX engine was bored out to 1258cc and fitted with 11:1 Cosworth pistons, driving a lightened and reworked standard Suzuki crank. Big Cosworth valves were operated by Megacycle cams, while extensive gas flowing of the head was enhanced by Egli's own free-flow exhaust system, and the powerplant was fed by a bank of 36mm Mikuni carburettors.

The engine produced 170lb-ft at the gearbox at 9200rpm, with 107lb-ft of torque at 7300rpm – just to prove the point, every bike sold had a record of its power output. To cope with the horsepower, the Suzuki five-speed gearbox was modified, and the standard clutch replaced by an American Barnett unit. The result was storming acceleration and a tested top speed of 174mph. If that wasn't enough, Egli also offered larger capacity versions of Red Lightning II.

Egli went on to offer more hyper-performance bikes, one being the Egli Turbo, a refined replica of the legendary MRD1. This used the Kawasaki four-cylinder engine in 1100 or 1200cc capacities, and weighed in at 212kg. With 180-250bhp available – depending on boost pressure – the performance was phenomenal, the bike reaching 124mph from a standing start in just 7.2 seconds. Egli built a record-breaking version, with the same engine, but higher boost and larger intercooler, which

The components which make up the Bonneville kit.

balanced crankshaft handled the power, which was transmitted to the rear wheel through a reinforced clutch. A special racing ignition system automatically retarded the spark in proportion to turbocharger boost pressure. As with most Egli performance engines, custom-built exhaust headers enhanced the efficiency of the whole setup.

Naturally, the bike used one of Egli's superb cantilever frames and his own front forks. The result is a machine with the stability necessary to cope with the immense power. But although the MRD1 Replica can be supplied with a dual seat, Egli does not recommend it!

Another of Egli's standard high performance bikes was the Bonneville. Again, this used a four-cylinder Kawasaki engine, in capacities of 750-1200cc. The frame was a nickel-plated backbone steel type, with cantilever rear swingarm controlled by a gas shock absorber. It was exactly the same frame layout as that used by Jacques Cornu to set a new lap record at the Nürburgring in 1981, beating works machines in the process, so the Bonneville was as at home on the track as it was on the road.

Although the Bonneville was a catalogued design, there was a long list of options, including wheels of different sizes and rim widths, race-bred brake components, selected instruments, alternative gear ratios, and much more.

The Red Hunter used a similar frame to the Bonneville, this time designed to accept Honda fours of 750-1200cc, all offered with Egli tuning. In conjunction with Shule, the German exhaust specialist, Egli developed a 4-2-1 exhaust system for the Honda four-cylinder engines, which produced an 8-10bhp increase in the medium rpm range, with a weight saving of 7.2kg.

showed 290bhp on the dyno and clocked 202.5mph at Nardo, southern Italy, with a top-half fairing only.

To achieve such outstanding performance, the internals of the Egli Turbo received considerable attention. Egli's own oil pump delivered 30 per cent more oil than the standard item, and there was an alcohol-water injection system. If required, N_2O injection could be fitted, resulting in 50 per cent more power. Specially forged pistons ran in Nikasil-coated aluminium cylinder liners, topped by modified cylinder heads. A perfectly

Due to the renewed interest of a large number of riders in single-cylinder engines in the 1990s, Egli produced an ultra-light sports single as well, the Red Falcon. The interesting point about this machine was that two standard versions were catalogued: one for a wet sump Honda engine, the other for a dry sump Yamaha, though it could be made to order with other single-cylinder engines.

Motorcycle Road & Racing Chassis

The famous Suzuki Red Lightning II. With its Egli-reworked engine, it was one of the fastest road-going production machines available.

Similar frames were used for both versions of the familiar nickel-plated, rigid backbone layout. As with all Fritz Egli motorcycles, the Red Falcon was offered with a wide range of chassis component options, while the engines could be supplied in any state of tune required, there being the usual range of special engine parts to enhance performance.

Apart from complete machines, Fritz Egli also catalogued a very wide range of special parts for both chassis and engines. From the chassis point of view, these included special wheels, brake components, forks and suspension parts, and much more. Engine parts included high performance pistons, crankshafts, oil pumps and cams. All had been developed over the years by Egli for use on customers' machines, or supplied separately for customers to carry out their own tuning work. And, of course, to finish the machine, there was always a range of fairing options.

The Enfield connection

For a manufacturer famous for such a wide range of high-performance motorcycles, Fritz Egli's latest business project of the early 1990s came as a bit of a surprise. He began to import Indian-built Royal Enfields.

The Madras factory has produced the Enfield Bullet range for a considerable number of years, and when Fritz discovered this he bought four bikes and ran them for a year to see how they performed. He was prompted to do this out of nostalgia, as the first motorcycle he owned had been a 350cc Bullet. Although the Indian-built Enfields had become popular, their build quality had

This one-off is a turbocharged Kawasaki-engined machine built for drag racing.

been criticised, but Fritz saw potential in this modern classic, believing that the problems could be eradicated and further improvements made.

So when he became the Swiss importer for Royal Enfield in 1992, he developed his own pre-delivery improvement programme for each machine sold. The frame was checked for straightness, and corrected it necessary, while the wheels and spokes were checked and trued-up where needed. The forks were stripped completely, all the components being deburred and polished. New dual-rate springs were ftted, together with special low-friction oil seals. The front drum brake was overhauled, and machined where necessary for roundness. Various options were available, such as different handlebars, alloy wheel rims and Koni adjustable rear shock absorbers.

The cylinder head and barrel were stripped, and the head flange machined to closely match the barrel, thus dispensing with the normal head gasket. This improved heat transfer and raised the compression slightly to 7:1. Valve seats were machined to line up accurately with the valve guides, and blended into the combustion chamber and ports. The valve spring seats were modified to give the correct height, while the rocker gear was ground to achieve correct alignment and to take out some weight.

The ignition system was reworked, a new carburettor manifold installed, and the carburettor itself fitted with a different slide and needle. An Egli high-output oil pump replaced the original.

The transmission (not the Bullet's best point) came in for attention as well. The gearbox is stripped, all parts being deburred and polished. A new bronze layshaft was bushed and fitted, while the gear selectors were engineered to achieve a smooth, reliable action. Gearing was altered to suit the particular model, and the clutch dismantled, the drum lining faces machined flat, the steel discs being slotted. Finally, everything was carefully reassembled.

Apart from producing an enjoyable and reliable machine, the Egli treatment

also improved the Bullet's performance. At the time, a standard Indian-built 500cc Bullet developed 22bhp, while the Egli version delivered 26bhp.

In addition to the improved Bullet, Fritz went on to offer two larger capacity versions. One was 535cc, being bored out from 84 to 87mm and using larger valves to improve breathing, while an alloy cylinder barrel (3kg lighter than standard) replaced the standard cast-iron cylinder. This 535 version of the Bullet produced 45bhp at 5100rpm.

To top the lot, Fritz sold the 624cc Super Bullet, which had the same mods as the 535, with the addition of a long-stroke crankshaft. It also ran a higher compression ratio of 8.9:1 – the stock compression is 6.5:1. The result was 47bhp at 5100rpm, with more torque throughout the rev range.

For those seeking the looks and ride of the classic era, these Indian-built, Egli-improved Enfields were bound to have an appeal, and this is borne out by the fact that Fritz sold 52 of them in the first year, with 90 machines projected for the following year. The better Bullet not only gave the bike world another interesting product, but it added another string to Fritz Egli's powerful and accurate bow.

Today, Fritz Egli maintains a strong business interest in

Egli's latest project is as an importer, and improver, of the classic-style Enfields from India. This example is the Bullet Classic Solo.

Motorcycle Road & Racing Chassis

motorcycles, but over the last few years his mode of operation has changed. He no longer produces in numbers the wonderful hand-built frames that won over many enthusiasts and made him famous worldwide.

The beautiful Egli-Vincents are an example. Frames and chassis were made by Fritz for other engines for both road and race use, but as time progressed Egli began to make more and more frames to house a variety of Japanese engines, starting with the Honda 750/4. Most of the chassis built by Egli during the 1970s were for Kawasaki Z900/Z1000 engines, though, over the years, many other engines have been used.

Fritz's original large diameter tube backbone chassis has proved to be so successful both for racing and road use, that it is still used today. From the beginning Egli used Ceriani or Marzocchi front forks, the rear suspension being taken care of by Koni, Ceriani, Girling or Betor shock absorbers. The braking was taken care of by Honda, Lockheed, Grimeca or Scarab parts, or indeed any other component the customer specified.

Fritz Egli's main business is now focused on maintaining the performance of customers' machines, including crash survey and repair, and the supply of a wide range of components for road or race use. He also imports MZ, Sachs, Royal Enfield, Rieju and Sherco to Switzerland, and has a dealer network for these products. One interesting sideline is the importation and modification of the Yamaha V-Max. He still maintains a strong interest in special builds if required, where his vast skills can be utilised. But the building of independent frame designs has been passed over to Patrick Godet in France whose work is fully endorsed by Fritz Egli. In fact, the quality of his work is such that Patrick, who builds his version of the Vincent-engined machines, has the blessing of Fritz to continue to use the Egli name. So the famous Egli-Vincents are still produced.

From Godet motorcycles of Sarl, there are several versions of the Egli-Vincent. The café racer is a machine for the real enthusiast, while the two-seater 'Sport GT' and the latest 'Tourer,' are aimed more at longer distance riders. All can be considered genuine Egli-Vincents.

Backbone of steel

Over the 20 years or so that Fritz Egli has been applying his considerable engineering talents to the production of motorcycles for race and road use, his reputation for both performance and finish has become legendary. Not only has he produced a wide range of machines for many uses, but he has also built very large numbers of some types. One would only have to attend an Egli owners' meeting to appreciate how popular and sought-after are the motorcycles from this long-established, independent frame maker.

The demand for Fritz Egli motorcycles is still strong worldwide, so these beautiful high-performance machines will continue to be produced for many years to come. Moreover, with Fritz Egli's continued enthusiasm, and his quest for performance and perfection from whatever engines become available, that demand is sure to continue.

An Egli transformation of the Harley-Davidson 'Lucifer's Hammer', 1993. (Courtesy Oli Tennent)

five

Harris Performance Products

As an independent motorcycle frame manufacturer, Harris Performance Products needs no introduction – its fame is worldwide and, for many years, it has built a wide variety of successful machines for many renowned riders. The business was formed in 1972 by two brothers, Steve and Lester Harris, both of whom served engineering apprenticeships.

Steve and Lester worked for different companies, but both on building race cars, Lester also being involved in the construction of go-karts. As the cars and karts of that period were tubular framed, the Harris brothers gained great experience in this form of construction, which was to prove invaluable later.

Although encouraged to race cars, the brothers turned to their first love, motorcycles. Both enjoyed successful club racing careers, which began on BSA A65s. Over the next few years, they found success on a variety of machines, including a Seeley G50, AJS 7R, Triumph Bonnevilles and, towards their later days of racing, TR500 Suzukis.

As enthusiastic club racers with

Harris is justly famous for the quality of its formed aluminium twin-spar chassis.

engineering backgrounds, the brothers carried out many modifications to their machines to improve performance, and the extent of these mods grew until eventually they began to build complete frames. Their work did not go unnoticed, and led to an increasing number of requests for similar modifications and frames from those less able to carry out this type of work themselves.

Motorcycle Road & Racing Chassis

This Triton replica frame was built in 1970 to house a Triumph twin, before the official formation of Harris Performance Products.

With full-time jobs, the brothers had difficulty finding the time to meet all these requests from other riders, never mind the requirements of their own racing programme. So they decided to give up the day jobs and form Harris Performance Products. The Harris brothers carried on racing for a further year, and this competition experience helped to get the company off to a good start. They began by making a variety of components, especially exhausts, though they would consider any part that differed from standard. This work became steady business, their reputation spread, and demand grew.

During this first year in business, Harris produced its first complete frame. This machine incorporated a feature that was considered advanced at the time: a monoshock (single rear shock absorber) which replaced the widely used twin shock system. Both frame and swing arm, as on all machines at the time, were built from steel tubing. This first complete Harris chassis housed a 250cc Suzuki Super 6 engine.

Lester Harris raced the Suzuki-powered machine for a season, but the engine's very narrow power band made it difficult to ride. Despite the engine proving unsuitable, the chassis delivered good handling. Other riders saw its worth, and orders for similar frames began to flow into Harris Performance Products.

In 1972, just after the company came into being, this complete chassis was made to house a Yamaha engine. Although it is of normal layout, note the early use of a single shock absorber.

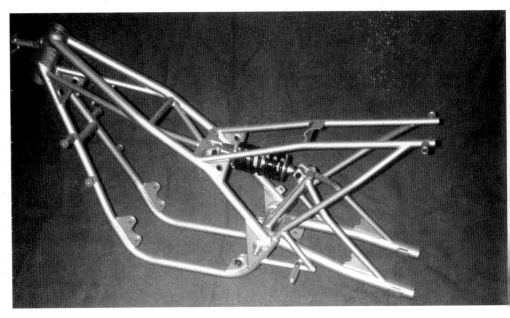

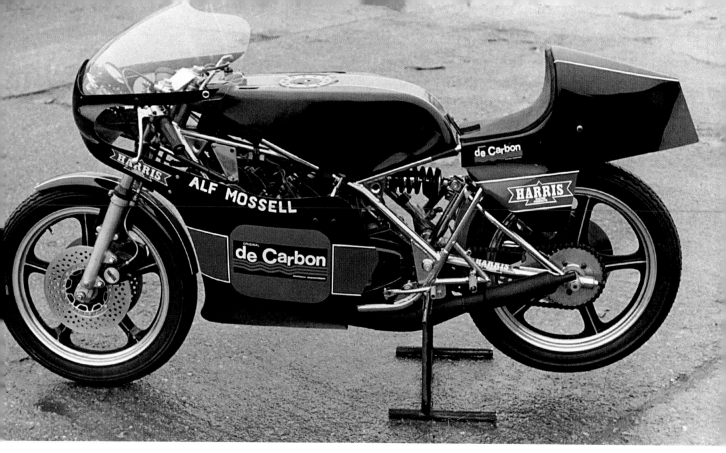

The completed TZ250 Yamaha-engined racer of 1972. The rider was a Harris employee.

This very first design was an instant success, and somewhere in the region of 15 were built. All were tailored to accommodate each customer's choice of engine, and these varied considerably. They included Triumph, Yamaha, Crescent and König. An interesting point is that both the Crescent and the König were developed from marine outboard engines, the Crescent being a three-cylinder design.

The Harris brothers' ability to design and build their own complete bike set the seal on their reputation, seen as the people to whom serious racers turned. This was illustrated by the number of their conversions of the very popular over-the-counter Yamaha TZ racer, from the standard twin shock absorber system to their state-of-the-art monoshock.

When the Harrises had been in full-time business for about two years, Steve Bayford joined the firm to handle the import and export of the very latest designs in cycle parts. After establishing and running this successfully for two years, he joined the Harris set-up as a full partner.

During the mid-1970s, the Yamaha TZ700 filled many entries in Formula 750 racing, but was considered by many not to handle too well in its standard form. Consequently, many riders asked Harris to fit the now proven monoshock system, and among those who took up this option for the 1976 season were Kork Ballington, Steve Parrish, John Newbold and Mick Grant. To illustrate the impact that the Harris rear end was having at the beginning of the European 750 Formula Championship, of the 32 starters on the grid for the first race at Silverstone, 18 used the Harris swingarm and monoshock.

In 1976-77, Barry Sheene won the world championship for Yamaha, and during 1978, the AKAI Yamaha that he was to ride was modified by Harris in an effort to improve its handling. This led to Harris building a complete chassis to house the Yamaha engine during the same season.

Back-to-back tests by Barry demonstrated that the Harris machine was better than the factory example, and he indicated that he wanted to use the machine. Yamaha offered him a full works machine, which had a new alloy chassis, but Sheene insisted on the works engine being fitted to the Harris chassis, and he got his way. This was very flattering for Harris and it proved to the world the esteem in which the company was held.

The following season, Barry Sheene was back with a brand-new works Yamaha for Grand Prix events, with the company's latest alloy chassis, though he continued to race a Harris chassis in the 750cc Superbike Championship, which had followed on from the 750cc European Championship. During that season, Sheene was involved in an horrific accident that resulted in both his legs being very badly smashed. While practising for the British Grand Prix, he ran into the bike of another rider who had

Motorcycle Road & Racing Chassis

fallen after taking a fast corner. So severe were Barry's injuries that the whole motorcycling world thought that his career was at an end. But he was so determined to carry on racing that within a few short weeks he signed a contract to ride for Suzuki. For a short spell he rode Randy Mamola's old machine, but Harris was contracted to build him a chassis, and continued to build frames for him until he retired. Although some exciting rides were to come from the Harris/Suzuki/Sheene combination, the best performance was third place in the South African Grand Prix of 1984, reflecting that by then the Suzuki engine was becoming dated.

While supplying Barry Sheene with Grand Prix chassis, Harris Performance was also becoming active in Formula 1. The company produced a chassis to house the Kawasaki Z1 900cc engine, which Andy Goldsmith and Mike Trimby raced successfully in endurance events. The success led to over 400 examples being produced for Formula 1, and between 1980 and 1985, many famous names were to ride Harris Formula 1

A tubular steel chassis built in 1974 to house the Suzuki TR750 engine. Note the concentric swingarm pivot.

Mike Trimby on 1975 Harris endurance racer.

bikes, including Phil Read, Mick Grant, Steve Parrish, Trevor Nation and John Newbold. During the early 1980s, Harris also found time to produce motocross chassis to house 250cc Suzuki engines for use in the World Championship by Suzuki UK.

The Formula 1 chassis built for Andy Goldsmith and Mike Trimby had a far-reaching effect on Harris, as it was the company's first excursion into the use of a four-cylinder engine, and the performance was impressive enough for Harris to develop a version for Martin Lunde, who raced it with considerable success during 1978-9. The machine was known as the Magnum, and it led to Harris Performance Products taking a very significant step forward.

The Magnum MkI.

Although competing against factory machines, the Magnum proved a serious contender, and resulted in a steady demand for racing versions. However, the obvious potential of this design as a high performance road bike was not overlooked by Harris. So the company built one, and it enjoyed a steady demand from road riders. The name Magnum is now firmly established, but the complete bike – in both race and road trim – has been much developed over the years.

The Magnum has been highly versatile, adapting to both road and track use. Its well-proven design, based on a fully-triangulated chassis made from Reynolds 531 steel tubing, manganese-bronze welded, forms the basis for a machine that can be supplied fully finished or in kit form, something that is unique for this class of machine. Harris offers a comprehensive service to the home builder by undertaking any of the assembly work that the customer cannot do. So no matter how the Magnum is purchased, it can be tailored to personal requirements.

The customer's donor bike supplies many of the major standard components that fit directly into the

Another Magnum MkI, built to a customer's specification.

This early 1980s photograph shows tester Harris handing over a Harris-built machine to its new owner. The engine is a 500cc Honda.

Magnum chassis. Any donor parts that are not suitable are replaced by those from the kit. Although the original Magnum was designed around a Kawasaki, there have been Yamaha-, Suzuki- and Honda-based versions.

During 1984-85, Suzuki UK contracted Harris to build machines that, in essence, were replicas of those built previously for Barry Sheene. Suzuki ran a two-bike team using these machines, the riders being Phil Mellor and Mark Phillips, but many were sold to many privateer racers, including Trevor Nation, Darren Dixon and Steve Manley, among whom it proved a lasting favourite. Mark Phillips won the 1987 British Championship on one, while Darren Dixon repeated the feat the following year. It was so popular that examples were still being raced in 1990.

Until the mid-1980s, Harris had concentrated on tubular steel frames, but by 1984-85 had made considerable advances in the development of an aluminium-alloy chassis, which went into production to accept a 250cc Rotax engine. The chassis incorporated two rectangular box-section alloy extensions that formed the main part of a twin-spar layout. Strength and stiffness were enhanced in critical areas by the addition of alloy sheet to form further box sections. An alloy rear swingarm of Harris design completed the rolling chassis.

The new design, built as a serious 250cc racer, was supplied to a company called Decorite, which commissioned Harris to design it. This company raced successfully in the 250cc class, but also very effectively marketed the machine under its own name, resulting in approximately 50 machines being built, a significant number for a pure race machine. By then, the alloy chassis was becoming state-of-the-art, and Harris continued to develop the use of the material.

Dr J Erlich was another customer who commissioned Harris to build a chassis, also designed to take the 250cc Rotax. Again, it was of the backbone type, using rectangular box-section extrusions with additional boxing where required. This chassis was completed with an alloy swingarm and became the 1985 MkI. Dr Erlich successfully raced a full team under the well-known designation of EMC, and Harris continued to

Jim Wells riding one of two Harris entries in the 1984 Formula 1 TT.

During 1983, Harris designed and built this Formula 1 chassis to house a 1000cc Kawasaki engine.

build for him, producing approximately 12 MkIs.

In its quest for improvement, Harris had begun to develop the technique of forming alloy sheet to the required box-sections and then welding them together. This enabled the chassis to be formed to the required shape and layout without the limitations imposed by standard extrusions. It also allowed the shape to be designed to enhance the structural performance. While this method of frame building gave more technical scope, it was much more difficult to carry out, and more expensive.

Although the EMC based on the

The frame arrangement of the 1983 Harris-built F1 machine.

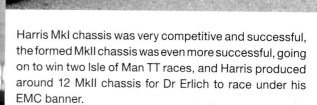

Harris MkI chassis was very competitive and successful, the formed MkII chassis was even more successful, going on to win two Isle of Man TT races, and Harris produced around 12 MkII chassis for Dr Erlich to race under his EMC banner.

In 1984 the Formula 1 engine capacity limit was reduced from 1000cc to 750. Harris designed and built machines to race in this formula, and also ran a two-bike

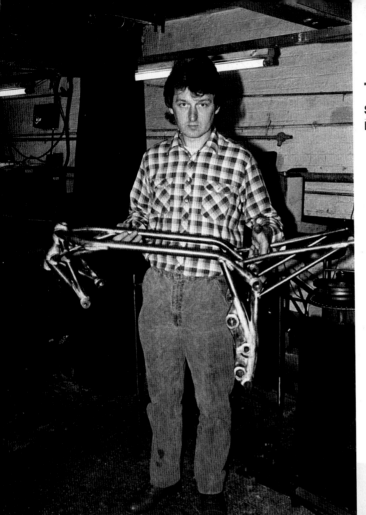

Steve Harris holds the frame for another F1 machine, built in late 1984 for a GPZ 750 Kawasaki.

team under its own name, the riders being Asa Moyse and Jim Wells. Although racing against factory teams, the Harris team achieved sixth place in the World Championship that year. On the whole, factory domination of Formula 1 was too strong for the private owners, which tended to spoil the class somewhat. Despite this, the Harris machine proved popular with the private teams, and approximately 50 were produced.

During the 1985 season, Harris ran a single-machine F1 team, the bike built around a Kawasaki GPZ 750R engine, the first Harris had built using a water-cooled, four-cylinder four-stroke. But despite a sterling effort from rider Asa Moyse, wins were not to come – the engine simply didn't have the power of its factory-backed adversaries. It was also too heavy, which had a serious effect on the power-to-weight ratio. But once again, the Harris chassis design proved popular with private teams and individuals, being seen as one of the best available. Something in the region of 35 were built, some having lighter, air-cooled engines.

The complete Kawasaki-based F1 machine.

During 1984-5, Harris designed and built an alloy chassis to house a Rotax 250. The work was carried out for a company called Decorite, which was to race the machine. Success on the track led to approximately 50 of these machines being sold. Note the use of extrusions and formed alloy components.

The Decorite 250 in action.

Motorcycle Road & Racing Chassis

A tubular steel frame under construction around an XBR 500cc Honda engine.

The complete Honda XBR-based machine.

Harris Performance Products

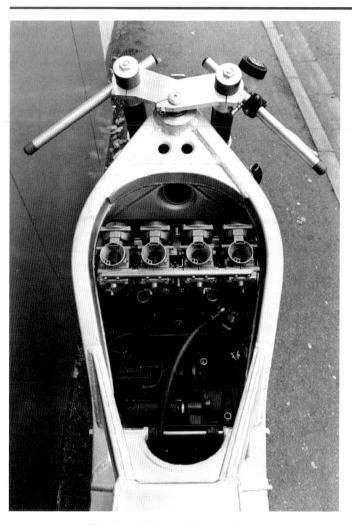

The Parrish frame in plan view.

The alloy chassis built for Steve Parrish with the three Harris partners. From left to right: Steve Harris, Steve Bayford, Lester Harris.

That same year, Harris produced an alloy chassis to house Yamaha's RD500 LC, a water-cooled two-stroke V4. It was based on a rectangular extrusion, boxed in strategic areas to achieve the required structural performance, and with riders like Steve Parish, Ron Storey, Des Barry, Clive Paget and Phil Mellor, success should have been assured. Sadly, the LC proved difficult to tune, while reliability was not its strong point, and a string of wins was not forthcoming.

In 1986 Harris made further improvements to the alloy-extrusion chassis for Steve Parrish, who raced it with the Yamaha FZ750 engine, another of the new generation water-cooled, four-stroke fours. A similar bike was raced by Matt Oxley and Vesa Kultalahti in endurance events, and they finished in a creditable sixth place in the World Championship. Harris had more involvement in endurance that year, after it was contracted by Tetsu Ikuzawa of Japan to produce a bike and run it in the Suzuka eight-hour race. They designed and built a chassis around the Honda VFR750, a combination that proved very competitive. This very prestigious endurance race attracted all the factory teams, who employed Grand Prix riders. However, the Harris entry, ridden by Trevor Nation, Graham McGregor and Ray Swan, ran in a very creditable seventh place until the closing stages when a pitstop dropped them back. Despite this, they still finished in a fine 12th place.

There was more endurance activity the following year, with Harris' first box-type chassis completely formed from alloy sheet. This lightweight, yet stiff design was built around the Yamaha FZ750 engine, although the same chassis was also made to

Motorcycle Road & Racing Chassis

accommodate the Kawasaki GPX750. This advanced design was to finish second in that year's World Championship, while another example came fifth. This was an outstanding performance in the face of the full factory teams, and the same design was modified to include the latest requirements for the 1988 endurance championship, and supplied to several private teams.

1986 had seen the inauguration of the Super Stock Formula, a series for production-based bikes. The rules for Super Stock decreed the use of production chassis, but modifications were allowed as long as the general layout or appearance remained the same. This form of racing quickly became popular, and Harris soon found its experience and skills in demand. The company modified Suzukis, Yamahas and Kawasakis for the formula, and Keith Heuwen, Kenny Irons and Steve Parrish, all rode Harris-modified Super Stock bikes. Work on Super Stock machines remains a steady part of the Harris workload.

During 1988, Harris developed another alloy chassis utilizing box-sections formed from alloy sheet. It was designed for the single-cylinder SOS class, Harris ran its own bike, powered by a Rotax 600cc engine. It was ridden by Asa Moyse with great success: he won the British National Championship in 1989, and came second in 1990, although another Harris-framed bike did actually win the Championship that year. Once again, a new racing formula proved very popular, and Harris was called on to produce chassis for a number of privateers. In addition to the Rotax-engined type, versions were also produced for Honda and Yamaha engines.

For 1990, Harris sponsored an entry in the British Open Championship, the machine being a Yamaha OWO 1. The obligatory production chassis was modified to improve performance, with Mark Phillips as the rider. The following year was

The machine on Steve Parrish's right is the complete alloy-chassis bike with the Yamaha FZ750 engine. Harris undertook the entire project.

An interesting project in 1986 was the 125cc MBA. Alloy extrusions were used for the backbone-type frame.

Harris Performance Products

with carbon fibre wheels offered as an option. This was all encapsulated in specially designed bodywork.

Six machines were built for the 1992 season, and all of them went to private teams, though the Padgets entry, ridden by Simon Buckmaster, was supported by Harris.

For the following season, Harris produced just three bikes, one of which was sold to a private entrant, with the

Two-seat version of the MkII Magnum.

an exciting one for Harris, when Yamaha offered to supply it with Grand Prix engines – YZR500 V4 two-strokes. Harris was to design and build the machines, which would be offered for sale to private buyers. Such direct co-operation with a major manufacturer's race technology was a major step forward for an independent frame maker.

The frame consisted of an aluminium delta box with a carbon fibre subframe to support the seat. The engine position was adjustable, as was the swingarm spindle position. The front forks were upside down Ohlins and braking was taken care of by AP six-piston calipers, the front brake disc being of carbon fibre, while the rear disc was steel. Marchesini wheels were fitted as standard,

A 1988 F1 machine based on a Suzuki GSX-R750 engine.

This complete machine was built around a 900cc Ducati engine.

Harris built a series of these machines for Laverda, the engine a 600cc twin. During 1987, this machine was voted the best under-750cc GT by *Das Motorrad* magazine.

Harris is prepared to go beyond pure engineering work, as this version of an aerodynamic fairing shows.

Motorcycle Road & Racing Chassis

The Harris-modified Yamaha OWO 1 for racing in the British National Championship.

Teamwork

Over the years, Harris Performance Products has designed and built machines for road and track, in both small numbers and relatively large production runs. However, this has not been the sole aim of the business. To this day, it maintains its ability for designing and building prototypes, as well as making many engineering improvements and modifications to existing bikes, coupled with the occasional rebuild.

The company has one major advantage in this business, in that most of the engineering processes required are available in-house. It employs top-class welders, fabricators and engineers, and also has its own GRP shop, so all bodywork is made in-house as well. These facilities, together with their obvious engineering talents, have served the Harris brothers well and have led to the excellent reputation they now enjoy worldwide.

There is one other ingredient that will keep Harris Performance Products in the forefront of independent motorcycle chassis builders for many years to come – enthusiasm, as strong now as it was in 1972, if not stronger.

The Harris story is one of many successes, but inevitably there have been mistakes, and things have gone wrong. With the benefit of hindsight, some of these events can seem funny now. One early customer, for example, wanted his chassis nickel-plated, which Harris arranged to have done. It was completed just in time for the company to spend the night building the bike into race trim, after which it was packed straight into a crate for transit to an overseas event. Three days later, at the distant circuit, the rider and the owner waited for the bike to be unpacked, having spread the word about the new machine. Proud Harris personnel were on hand to accept any credit. However, when the crate was opened, there was a stony silence. Inside, there was no gleaming nickel-plated racing chassis; instead, the bike was covered in what appeared to be green fungus.

Another amusing episode occurred when the Harris team travelled to an overseas circuit with a van, a car and a caravan. As the caravan wasn't needed until they arrived, they had filled it with GRP fairings, which were to be sold from the paddock as a means of subsidising the racing. The unfortunate driver towing the caravan did not know about the fairings until a punctilious customs officer pointed them out. He spent a short time in the local cells, but that wasn't the end of the story. On arrival at the circuit, the team began to sell the fairings. At the time, these were unobtainable on the continent, so a good profit was considered possible. Since the cost was £15, a selling price of £30 was settled on; but a strange thing happened. Instead of

other two run as a full works team sponsored by Shell. The riders were Sean Emmelt and Andrew Stroud.

The unique aspect of the Harris/Yamaha project was that it allowed private teams to buy machines to compete at Grand Prix level. Moreover, they could opt for a service contract, which meant that the bike would be serviced at all the race meetings by Harris technicians. This included frame re-jigging and welding, along with a comprehensive spares back-up, even to the extent of a spare engine should that be needed.

The Harris Grand Prix machines put in some very creditable performances against the might of the factory teams, culminating in Terry Rymer's sixth place in the 1992 British Grand Prix. The results achieved in the first two seasons were not sensational, but they did show that an independent manufacturer can produce competitive Grand Prix machinery.

The Magnum MkIII, finished to a customer's specification.

selling individually, they began to sell in batches of ten or more. The mystery was solved later in the day, when it was discovered that the fairings were being re-sold for £60 each at stalls outside the paddock. Harris learnt a valuable lesson about market research that day.

Steve Bayford recalls a moment, just after he joined Harris as a partner. A friend, who had been told that Steve was working for a company that made racing motorcycles, would phone him and open the conversation by saying, "Barry Sheene here, can you make me a couple of bikes?" At the time, Barry Sheene was the biggest name in bike racing, but Steve's unprintable reply always came quickly off the tongue. Then one day Steve picked up the phone and a voice said, "Barry Sheene here. My bike won't handle. Would you consider building me one?" Steve's reply was "You can't handle your women, so I'm not surprised you can't handle your bike!" Fortunately, Mr Sheene took it in good part, and that call led to a long and successful association.

It was during 1992 that Harris had its first full year of the

This superb restoration of an MV Agusta demonstrates the versatility of Harris Performance Products.

The Harrier 3 uses a Harris frame designed for the Triumph triple.

Shell Harris GP Team, the riders being Sean Emmet, James Haydon and Neil Hodgson. At the same time, Harris was to start producing bikes for the Supermono class of racing, and would see success in this class with a TT victory and a British Championship. Jim Moodie was the rider for the TT win and Dave Rawlings took the British title.

During all the racing activity Harris continued to produce its very wide range of motorcycle parts, and service both racing and road going machines. It was during the early 1990s that Harris received the ultimate compliment of being one of the only two companies world-wide to be licensed by Yamaha Japan to buy factory race engines, these being housed in the Harris designed and built chassis that would compete in the Blue Riband 500cc Grand Prix World Championship.

The massive effort made by Harris to compete with the factory teams was not to go unnoticed. By the 1995 season

Harris Performance Products

Shown here is the Harris WCM Moto GP machine.

These photographs show the Harris Sauber Moto GP bike.

Motorcycle Road & Racing Chassis

Harris was the biggest individual team, with three GP riders. This not only drew wide media attention, but also that of Suzuki, which invited Harris to create, organise and manage the official Suzuki World Superbike Team, racing its latest flagship, the GSX-R750WT. Suzuki also contracted Harris to distribute the factory race kit components to Suzuki Superbike customers.

As a result of that, Harris was instrumental in the GSX-R's development into a formidable race winner at all levels of the sport, during the 1996/7/8 seasons. The years 1999 and 2000 saw Harris maintain its association with World Championship racing. The company's hands on approach was utilised during 1999 with involvement with the Kawasaki Motors UK Superbike team. The following year Harris began the formation and running of the Harris Honda British Superbike team, which resulted in the development of the VTR1000 SP-1. The company also became involved in racer training, to help and promote young Superbike riders.

During 2001 Harris was invited by Sauber Petronas Engineering AG to join it as its chassis partner, a reflection of the esteem in which the company was held for its now well established design and development skills. The aim of this partnership was to develop a four-stroke Grand Prix racer utilising the SPE-developed engine, and the first phase of this project culminated in a completely new racer being presented at the 2001 Malaysian Motorcycle Grand Prix.

This association with SPE was maintained throughout 2002. On top of this commitment and its continuing expansion of its parts production, Harris moved to new premises during this period. During 2002 Harris was approached by WCM to design, build and develop a Moto GP machine, to accommodate an engine the latter was to develop. But involvement in this rarified sector of racing didn't allow Harris to forget its roots, and the company remains a one-stop shop for sports bike riders and racers alike, where you can buy everything from a screen to a complete frame kit.

Harris/Yamaha Grand Prix machine minus its
bodywork.

Illustrated here is the Harris Magnum 4 frame sporting a normal type of twin-side swingarm rear suspension.

A Harris Magnum 4 fitted with a single leg rear suspension.

An example of the Harris Magnum 5 frame.

Harris Performance Products

A complete Harris Magnum 5 with a twin-sided swingarm.

Another Magnum 5, this one with a single-sided swingarm.

six

Hejira Racing HRD

Hejira is an unusual name for a very British business, but the translation explains it all. Hejira is Arabic for 'to fly', and the performance record of the machines from this company justifes that name.

Hejira designs and builds racing motorcycle frames, and has chosen to concentrate in this area. However, some of its frames, built to house larger engines, have been used in the construction of road machines.

The man behind Hejira, Derek Chittenden, was born with competition blood coursing through his veins. His father was an avid grass track racer, and Derek followed in his footsteps, although his will to compete took him into other forms of motorcycle sport. One that he pursued very strongly was motocross, before he took to road racing. Maintaining the family tradition, Derek's eldest son now designs and builds Hejiras, while his youngest son has taken up motocross.

Derek Chittenden's competitive spirit made him reluctant to drop one type of racing to pursue another and, in fact, his experiences on one bank holiday weekend are unlikely to be equalled by many, let alone beaten. He competed in a grass track

Derek Chittenden, in 1977, on a bike based on one of his own Hejira motocross frames. During this early period, motocross was Derek's favoured sport; road racing was to come later.

Hejira Racing HRD

The first prototype road racing frame built by Derek Chittenden at the end of 1973. It housed a 250cc Ducati engine. Although bearing the Hejira name, it was actually built before the company had been formed.

experience in satisfying demand. Then in 1974, Derek took a significant step by building his first road race frame. This housed a 250cc Ducati engine, and it was built for a rider who had the good sense to think that Derek's skill should be extended beyond motocross frames.

That first road race frame lived up to expectations and resulted in orders for further examples and, during 1975, Derek built four more of them. Again, these machines used Ducati's

A 1979 Hejira road racing frame for 250 and 350cc engines. Note the use of round-section steel tubing.

meeting on the Friday, took part in a road race on the Saturday, then rode in a motocross meeting on the Monday – not bad for an amateur club competitor.

Motocross was the sport on which Derek began to concentrate, however, and the more involved he became, the more he found the need to have a bike built to suit his personal needs. This is where his engineering skills, gained through an apprenticeship with British Rail, proved to be more than useful. Derek had carried out the inevitable modifications to existing machines which, in turn, led to the manufacture of a complete motocross frame, which he built during 1960. Over the next few years, more frames were built, as other motocross riders wanted to benefit from his skills, and Derek gained a lot of useful

250 single, and together with some friends, Derek ran two of these bikes as a team. Two seasons later, in 1977, he built four more road race frames, this time housing an AJS Stormer 250cc two-stroke single.

The amazing thing about Derek Chittenden's frame building is, at that point in his career, all the work had been carried out

Steve Cull on a 600cc Hejira Ducati during the 1983-4 season. He finished ninth in the F2 race on the Isle of Man.

as a hobby on a part-time basis. He even found time to compete on motorcycles himself, but the time had come to decide what to do about this time-consuming hobby. His frames had performed well in Clubman racing, and their growing reputation led to a demand for frames from other enthusiasts. So Derek decided to take the plunge, turning his hobby into a full-time business.

In 1978, Hejira Racing HRD Ltd was born. Derek had chosen the company name several years before, and all the machines he had built prior to that date had carried the Hejira name. Consequently, a useful reputation had been built upon which the company could begin to trade.

In fact, the new company was a partnership between Derek Chittenden and Danny Wilson, though, in 1989, ill health caused Danny to pull out of Hejira, and he went his own way.

The development prototype of the hub-centre steering machine.

Richard Hunter on a 1982 Hejira Suzuki. Richard finished in an excellent second place in the F3 TT on the Isle of Man.

Hejira Racing HRD

A serious-looking Derek Chittenden with a Hejira Ducati in 1984.

The first frame built by the new company housed a 250cc twin-cylinder Suzuki engine, which led to further work in the 250 class, a very competitive formula that lends itself to frame development. Derek Chittenden's experience and proven ability made him a prime candidate to fill the needs of the competitors in this area.

Hejira was soon very busy, designing and building frames for Suzuki, Yamaha, Rotax and Sach engines, all of them racing 250s. In fact, in this outstanding season, Hejira built over 30 racing frames, which in racing terms is a lot of machines. This type of work continued over the next two seasons, mainly for the 250cc racing formula.

Up to this point, all the frames designed and built by Derek used round steel tubing, but during 1981, he made the transition to square-section steel tubing, and he still advocates the use of steel tubing when conventional methods of frame making are employed. Apart from that change to square-section tubing, his method of frame building hasn't changed for 30 years. Obviously, it was right in the first place.

All Hejira frames feature the company's own rear swingarm, again built from welded steel tubing. As each swingarm is designed to meet the specific needs of the frame, the section of the tubing used will be selected to achieve the required performance. Front forks usually come from a major fork manufacturer, selected to achieve the best results. Years of racing, building and preparing competition bikes has given Derek Chittenden a wealth of experience when it comes to selecting the best components to do a particular job – shock absorbers, brakes, electrics and engine parts. Like most race bike builders, Derek Chittenden has considerable expertise in the last area, particularly the all-important exhaust system.

In 1982, Hejira widened its horizons, building its first frame for the Rotax 500cc four-stroke single. It led to further orders for this type of frame, as the single-cylinder formula was gaining popularity.

Although still a comparatively small company, it entered into a busy programme of building racing frames for both 250 and 500cc single formulae. Despite this, it also managed to produce frames for other engines and formulae. Frames were built to house engines from 750 to 1100cc. In the main, these were four-cylinder powerplants from Suzuki, Kawasaki and Honda. Most of these machines were built for the various formulae operated at national club level, but some frames were supplied to customers who completed their machines for road use.

It would have appeared that this energetic and enthusiastic frame maker had enough to keep him busy, having established a wide base of capabilities to ensure continued business. However, Derek Chittenden was about to surprise the motorcycling fraternity with another innovative project.

During 1983, on top of all the other Hejira work, he designed and built a complete machine that featured hub-centre steering. Although it was not the first hub-centre steering frame ever produced, it was certainly a bold and advanced project for such a small company.

Unlike some hub-centre steering projects, which used the engine as a stressed member of the frame, the Hejira version had a full centre section. In other words, it was a complete rolling chassis even without the engine. One major advantage of this arrangement was that the chassis could be made to accept almost any engine, or range of engines.

Derek Chittenden's design used square-section steel tubing in the construction of the frame and the upper front suspension wishbone, with sheet steel employed to fabricate a large deep-section backbone. Larger rectangular sections were used for the single leading leg of the front suspension, and for the conventional Hejira rear swingarm.

Another interesting aspect of this machine was its fabricated front wheel, designed and made by Hejira to meet the need for an offset wheel to accommodate the single-leg front suspension. The wheel consisted of a steel disc centre bolted to a flanged rim. To achieve the offset, long spacers were fitted between the rim flange and the centre. A large-diameter, single front brake disc was mounted within the offset wheel. As a conventional swingarm was used, the rear wheel was a normal off-the-shelf item.

Many test miles were covered by this interesting prototype, but the lack of a development budget prevented its potential being realised. The prototype is still retained by Hejira and may be developed further if resources allow, or its technology may be used for other machines in the future.

Over the next few seasons, Hejira continued to construct the frames on which it had built its reputation, as well as making continual modifications to customers' machines. On top of this, it ran a works racing team in the singles formula, which, in 1986, moved from 500 to 600cc, though this didn't necessitate any frame changes

In 1991 another advanced design was under way at Hejira. For this project, Derek Chittenden was investigating the potential of the very latest in materials technology.

Carbon fibre was used as the main structural material for both the frame and rear swingarm, while some aerospace-type honeycomb was used strategically to enhance the performance in specific areas. This exciting project was a joint effort between Derek Chittenden and Max Powell. Derek's experience of what was required from the frame was fulfilled by Max, who took care of the composite aspect.

The resultant frame was of a backbone type except that, unlike the normal twin-spar layout, the spar sides were joined together at the rear in similar fashion to the steering head area. Integral extensions carried the swingarm pivots. To achieve this very impressive arrangement, carbon fibre prepreg materials, suitable for the structural requirements, were moulded at high temperature in a vacuum. Carbon fibre materials were moulded in the same way to produce the all-composite swingarm. Bearing housings, such as those for the steering head and the swingarm, were machined metallic components bonded onto the moulded carbon fibre parts as a secondary operation.

Composites have many advantages over conventional materials in motorcycle frames. In most cases, they are lighter but just as strong, which can be achieved by the selection of specific materials, and enhanced in particular areas by the orientation of the material fibres for maximum strength. Extra material need only be added where more strength is required. In this way, structural performance can be optimized without the addition of unwanted weight.

Designing and manufacturing in composites is a somewhat

Left to right: Derek Chittenden, Martin Bartlett (the rider), and Danny Wilson (Derek's partner in the early years of Hejira). The machine is a Hejira 250 twin. This photograph was taken in 1986, during the British Championship round at Silverstone.

different operation to working with conventional materials. Varying performances can be achieved with the same material, depending on the method used, so composite structures are more individual than those made from, say, steel, which is why there is no detailed technical information on the Hejira carbon fibre frame. However, Hejira did build a second bike alongside it, with a conventional tubular steel frame, that served as a useful comparison – the carbon fibre frame is both lighter and stiffer.

Since production of race frames began, Hejira has produced over 400 in differing categories, and the continuation of the design and building of race and road frames is still very much the aim of Derek Chittenden and Hejira.

By 1992, Hejira was using advanced technology to produce this carbon fibre frame and swingarm. The machine, which was equipped with a 600cc Rotax engine, was raced by the company.

Over the last few years the company has continued its use of carbon fibre composite materials. Its carbon fibre frame has been perfected along with a carbon fibre swingarm, and samples have been built to house different engines. Another major step in the use of carbon fibre has been the development of both front and rear wheels for racing motorcycles. Seats, fairings and other carbon components have also been added to the company's repertoire.

Another major step for Hejira has been the development and construction of its own engine. It has for some time developed and manufactured internal engine components, and this led to the development of a complete engine.

Still under development in 2007, it was a fuel-injected single with twin overhead camshafts, which could be produced in capacities from 450cc to 660cc. The engine and its components were machined from solid billet, and in race tune, the 660cc version was expected to produce 90bhp at 9000rpm. It was intended as a purely competition engine, and could open a new chapter in Hejira's development as a business.

Having developed exhaust systems, cooling systems and suspensions, and a full range of carbon fibre components, Hejira continues to be the progressive company that it was from the beginning, and holds its place among those independent motorcycle frame makers that have pioneered some aspects of motorcycle technology.

Motorcycle Road & Racing Chassis

This 1992 photograph shows the Hejira Team HRD racing machines after taking second and fourth places at a race in Holland.

This steel frame was designed to take big single cylinder engines, and is used in Supermono racing.

Hejira Racing HRD

This machine is a Suzuki RG500 engine in a Hejira carbon fibre frame, complete with carbon fibre wheels.

This is a Hejira GP 605cc race bike. Carbon fibre was used in the manufacture of the chassis, wheels, fuel tank and bodywork.

Hejira and Team HRD during the 1996 season.

Motorcycle Road & Racing Chassis

Hejira carbon fibre race wheel.

Hejira produces a wide range of parts. Shown here is an exhaust system for a 916 Ducati.

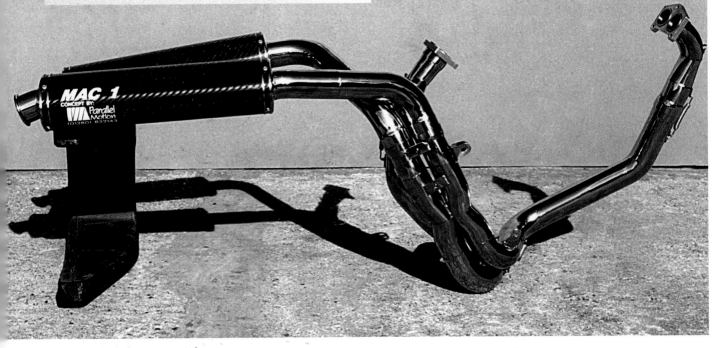

Visit Veloce on the web – www.velocebooks.com
New book news • Gift vouchers • Details of all books in print • Newsletter

seven

Magni

Magni is well-known in the motorcycle world for two good reasons: its connections with one of the world's most famous motorcycle factories, MV Agusta, and the excellent reputation it has achieved for the exciting motorcycles it has produced in its own right.

The company's founder, Arturo Magni, had what can only be described as a dream start to his career with motorcycles. This came

about in 1947, when he joined the racing department of Gilera. During this period, he was involved in the assembly of the famous Gilera four-cylinder engines, a background which was to prove invaluable. To extend this experience further, he moved to MV

An example of the first complete motorcycle produced by Magni: the MH1. A Honda 900cc four-cylinder engine is utilized, along with the donor bike's front forks and wheels. The MH2 made use of the engine alone and was fitted with a full fairing.

Motorcycle Road & Racing Chassis

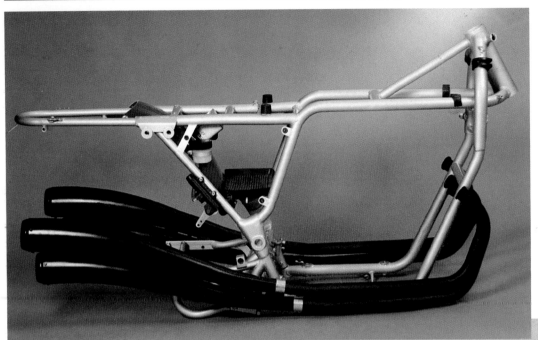

All early frames built by the company were similar to this example, which is designed to accept a four-cylinder MV Agusta unit.

kits, fairings, saddles, and special exhaust systems. But it wasn't long before they designed and began to manufacture the first frame to bear the Magni name. This was designed to house the four-cylinder MV Agusta engine, which is not surprising considering the connections at hand.

An early 1980s MB2 with a 1000cc BMW boxer engine.

Agusta, taking up a position in its racing department.

Arturo Magni eventually became chief of the MV Agusta racing department and remained in this position until MV withdrew from competition. He was responsible for motorcycles raced by the most famous riders of that period, admired to this day, such as Agostini, Surtees and Hailwood. To give an indication of the challenge laid down by the combination of these riders and MV Agusta machines, when the MV factory ceased racing it had won 75 World Championships.

The experience gained over 20 years in some of the world's greatest racing departments was too valuable an asset to waste, so, in 1977, a factory was opened by Arturo Magni and his sons, who between them set about building a family business. In the beginning, the new business produced special parts for MV Agusta machines: chain conversion kits, cylinder and piston

This vast experience and skill resulted in Magni producing parts for the four-cylinder MV engine as well, which enabled enthusiasts to restore four-cylinder MVs, and even build copies of the MV Agusta racers.

A few years later, Magni produced the first complete motorcycle to bear its name. This machine was based on Honda's

Magni's parallelogram rear suspension system. This provided shaft drive with the feel of a normal chain drive by eliminating transmission reaction. Other manufacturers have since copied this idea.

900cc four-cylinder engine, in Bol d'Or spec. Two versions were produced: the MH1 and MH2. The former utilized some of the original Honda parts, such as wheels and front forks, and was supplied without a fairing. The MH2 was a complete machine with a full fairing and using only the engine from the original Honda motorcycle. It proved very popular, somewhere in the region of 300 being produced.

During 1982-83, Magni designed and built a new frame to house a totally different type of engine: the 1000cc BMW flat-twin. Again, two versions were available, one being a basic model designated the MB1, the other (the MB2) being the flagship, with all the Magni-manufactured components, including a full fairing set.

Although this proved a popular machine, Magni was only able to produce about 150 examples because BMW introduced the K-series, and the Boxer engine went out of production.

From the very beginning, Magni has striven to give the customers what they want. Hence the continual changes in styling, as well as technical advances. An example of this awareness of what was needed was the Le Mans model, introduced during the first half of the 1980s. It boasted a full fairing of modern design, similar in style to those of the big-selling Japanese machines, while the technical specification was similarly up to date, particularly in the use of a parallelogram rear suspension system. This arrangement, designed by Magni, gave the machine a completely new feel. All the transmission reactions were eliminated, the shaft-drive system having the feel of a normal chain-drive transmission. Other motorcycle manufacturers, including BMW, have since utilized this system.

The left-side view of the parallelogram suspension.

Although marketed in 1987, the Classico was built with 1970s styling. It proved a popular model.

In 1987 the company chased the market with two new models: the Classico and the Arturo. Again, these were examples of Magni's innovation, although the styles were reminiscent of motorcycles of the 1970s. They had spoked wheels, 1970s-style mudguards, large round headlights, and a lack of bodywork, except in the case of the Arturo, which had a small half-fairing.

Although the machines appeared to be a retrograde step, their 1970s styling proved very popular, especially as they were built to the usual high Magni standard, all the components and accessories being of the very best quality.

The success of the Classico and Arturo models led Magni into taking the theme even further when, in 1989, it produced the Sfida, which was designed in the style of 1960s

Magni Le Mans, first seen at the Milan show in November 1985, with a choice of 948 or 1116cc Moto Guzzi engines. The first Magni machine was offered complete, and not as a frame kit.

An example of the Sfida. This particular version uses a 1000cc Moto Guzzi engine.

motorcycles, and powered by Moto Guzzi's 949cc V-twin. Again, spoked wheels were used, and an aluminium fuel tank of the period was reproduced.

The Sfida is still being produced at the time of writing, as the fuel-injected 1100, with four valves per cylinder, and over 500 examples have been sold. Magni is still producing the Arturo, this too with the eight-valve Moto Guzzi twin. In 1990, Magni launched a new race bike to compete in twin-cylinder road racing. It was so successful that a road version was launched in 1993, the Australia, and this too is still in production.

Although Magni produced its first machines based on the four-cylinder MV Agusta engine over 30 years ago, it continues to build machines with this engine. If a customer supplies an old MV Agusta or even just an engine, Magni will build a machine to the customer's requirements. This can be a complete restoration to original specifications, or the engine housed in a Magni frame. The resultant bike can be a performance road bike or a full classic racer.

A complete range of parts is available to meet the required specification: big carburettors, tuned exhaust systems, fuel tanks, wheels, fairings, and, of course, Magni designed suspension.

More recently, Moto Guzzi has also come in for the Magni treatment. A complete machine will usually have a change of suspension, wheels, fuel tank, seat, fairing and anything else the customer wants. Different Moto Guzzi engines are available, and Magni builds exciting road machines around any of them. Both 992cc and 1064cc V-twins are offered in four-valve or latest eight-valve fuel-injected form.

This ability to build a bike to the customer's spec means that few Magni Guzzis are the same, but a typical high performance road bike would have a specification as follows: Magni-designed and built frame; air-cooled 1064cc V-twin; compression ratio 9.5 to 1; induction by Weber Marelli electronic injection, two injectors fed by electronic fuel pump; full digital electronic management system; five-speed gearbox fitted with straight-cut gears; upside down forks, fully adjustable; Magni licenced rear

Motorcycle Road & Racing Chassis

A 1993 Magni Australia with 1000cc Moto Guzzi engine. (Courtesy Oli Tennent)

The Australia model in full race trim. Both Australia models make use of the 1000cc Guzzi V-twin.

shock, fully adjustable, with parallelogram linkage; twin 320mm front discs with 4-piston calipers; single rear 230mm disc with 2-piston caliper. The end result would weigh 190kg and have a claimed top speed of around 150mph.

Another exciting machine produced by Magni uses the Suzuki GSX1200 engine, hence the designation Magni Sport 1200S. This four cylinder air-cooled engine runs under a

9.5 to 1 compression ratio, with carburettor induction. Power is transmitted via a five-speed gearbox, all housed in a Magni frame. With all the usual Magni high performance suspension and brake gear, this results in a high-powered machine weighing in at 196kg, though the company doesn't disclose a maximum speed.

Magni has now been producing motorcycles for 30 years

Motorcycle Road & Racing Chassis

and is still producing mouth watering machines. The founder of the company, Arturo Magni, has now retired and left his very experienced son Giovanni to run the business. This will ensure that the demand and supply of these top class motorcycles will continue for many years to come.

Power and style

Magni's business has been built on giving the motorcycle world what it wants in terms of performance, styling and quality of build. All Magni tubular steel frames are built from 25 CROMO 4 tubing, argon welding being used to achieve the required structural performance. The number of machines that have been built since the company began gives a good indication of the quality of design and manufacture.

Although Magni produced its first machines based on the four cylinder MV Augusta engine over twenty-five years previously, it continues to build machines with this engine.

If a customer supplies an old MV Augusta bike, or even just an old engine, Magni will build a machine to the customer's requirements. This can be a complete restoration to original specifications, or the engine housed in a Magni frame. The bike can be a performance road bike or a full classic racer.

A full range of parts is available to meet the required specification; large carburettors, tuned exhaust systems, fuel tanks, wheels, fairings and, of course, Magni designed suspension.

Another make of machine to get the Magni treatment is Moto Guzzi. A complete machine will usually have a change of suspension, wheels, fuel tank, saddle, fairing and anything else to meet the customer's requirements. There are different Moto Guzzi engines available. Magni builds exciting road going machines round all versions. The available engine versions are a 992cc running under a 10.5 to 1 compression ratio and a 1064cc engine running under 9.5 to 1 compression ratio which are available with technical variations to suit customer requirements, these variations relating to bore and stroke compression ratio, induction systems, number of valves, etc.

The machines into which any of the Moto Guzzi engines are fitted will be built to the well known Magni standard resulting in an exciting machine built to do what is required of it. As previously stated the frame specifications together with the engine specifications are available to the customer's requirements, but a typical high performance road machine based on one of the Moto Guzzi engines would have a specification as follows – engine Moto Guzzi V twin air cooled of 1064cc capacity, compression ratio of 9.5 to 1, induction by Weber Marelli electronic injection, two injectors being fed by electronic fuel pump. A full digital electronic management system controls the electrics. This, together with a five speed gearbox fitted with straight cut gears is housed in

a Magni designed and built frame. Upside down forks, which would have hydraulic regulation in extension and jam, take care of the front end. Rear suspension is taken care of by the pre-loaded rear oscillating arm motivating force double to parallelogram, a Magni licensed shock absorber with hydraulic regulation in jam and extension and a regulated pre-loaded motivating force. Two 320mm discs with 4 hydraulic pistons take care of the front braking, the rear has a single 230mm disc with two brake pistons.

All this in a finished Magni machine would weigh 190kg and produce a top speed of 240km per hour.

Another exciting machine produced by Magni utilises the Suzuki GSX1200 engine designated Magni Sport 1200S. The four cylinder air-cooled engine runs under a 9.5 to 1 compression ration, induction is by carburettor. Power is transmitted via a five-speed gearbox, all housed in a Magni frame. With all the usual Magni high performance suspension and brake gear, this results in a high-powered machine weighing in at 196kg and capable of satisfying the most demanding of sporting motorcycle enthusiasts. No maximum speed was disclosed for this model.

Magni has now been producing motorcycles for over twenty-five years and are still producing mouth watering machines. This bears testament to the skill and quality that goes with Magni motorcycles.

With their skill and known build quality and the very wide range of technical ability, almost any motorcycle requirement can be met. The variations are endless, with suspensions, frames,

A Magni machine with the famous MV Augusta four-cylinder engine.

exhausts, ignition and induction systems, electronics, fairings etc., all available to build the machine to meet the customer's requirements,

Magni is one company that produces motorcycles for the children of motorcycle enthusiasts. This is its Minimoto, which is a replica of the famous MV Augusta four-cylinder racer. The Minimoto houses a 49.8cc single cylinder 2-stroke engine.

The founder of the company, Arturo Magni, has now retired and left his very experienced son Giovanni to run the business. This will ensure that the demand and supply of top class motorcycles will continue for many years to come.

Motorcycle Road & Racing Chassis

This is the Magni Sport 1200 with the 1200cc Suzuki four-cylinder engine.

A Magni Minimoto, which is a replica of the famous MV Augusta, scaled down and using a 49.8cc engine.

This Le Mans I Moto Guzzi is shown after a rebuild by Magni.

A Magni rebuilt Le Mans III Moto Guzzi. remodelled to customer requirements.

eight

Maxton Engineering

Maxton Engineering and Ron Williams are one and the same, and need little or no introduction in the world of motorcycle competition, having designed and built a wide range of racing chassis for a variety of users, including factory teams. Ron is a very talented designer and builder of racing motorcycle chassis and suspensions.

Ron left school at 16 and began an engineering apprenticeship, going on to work as a draughtsman with AEI. In 1966, with experience added to his engineering training, he joined Chevron Cars as its chief draughtsman. There, he designed Cosworth and BMW-powered single-seater and sports car chassis for a variety of formulae, including F3 and F5000.

All his technical knowledge and practical experience, coupled with a love of competition motorcycles, led Ron into building and racing his own sprint machine in his spare time. This was a successful venture, and he took several world records for both standing and flying starts.

During this very busy period, Ron had also become very interested in suspension systems, which led to the design and construction of a shock absorber testing machine for Chevron. But you can't keep a good motorcyclist down, and an essential part of this machine was a Norton gearbox.

Although engaged in competition car work, Ron was becoming increasingly interested in the new breed of motorcycle coming into England, powered by two-stroke engines. His interest

An example of the machines built by Maxton for the Dugdale team.

Motorcycle Road & Racing Chassis

was heightened by the problems the new type of engine brought with it. Handling and reliability could be suspect, associated in many cases with vibration caused by the high-revving motors. The challenge they offered was too great to resist and, in 1971, after five years with Chevron, Ron resigned. He had decided to design and manufacture frames to house these new and exciting engines.

The first cantilever frame built by Maxton Engineering in 1975. This was to prove very successful.

The workshop of Ron's enterprise was the garage attached to his parents' house. During his first year, he built six frames of steel tube construction, and the success of these first six was evident. The next year, he built over 20 frames, and this level of production was maintained for some years after. It was an impressive output when you consider that he did not employ anyone else, and carried out all the main construction work himself, only a minimum of work being sub-contracted.

After a few years, Ron was able to purchase a disused Methodist chapel, which was turned into a purpose-built workshop, and this was to become the home of the now well known Maxton Engineering.

During this period, all the frames from Maxton Engineering were of steel tube, designed and built by Ron himself. In addition to the many frames for club racers, he also built machines for riders of great experience who were competing all over the world.

This Maxton machine has been fitted with an extra-large fuel tank so that it can complete four full laps of the Isle of Man. It was ridden by Steve Carthy.

Maxton Engineering

Various stages in the construction of the frame built by Ron Williams to house the Honda NR500 oval-piston engine. This was constructed in the UK and shipped to Japan for evaluation.

In 1974, Maxton Engineering took a significant step forwards by working for Suzuki. This collaboration with a major Japanese manufacturer illustrates the respect which which the skills of Ron Williams and Maxton Engineering were held. Maxton Engineering built a chassis which, in essence, was a forerunner of the RG500. It was raced by Paul Smart in the 1974 British Grand Prix, followed by the remainder of the world's GPs that year.

Maxton built chassis for 250 and 350cc Grand Prix machines, in addition to examples for the Isle of Man TT races and the Manx. During 1975, Maxton supplied chassis for bike dealers Dugdale to race in the Manx GP series. Dugdale's confidence in Maxton Engineering and Ron Williams was to prove extremely rewarding, for the team went on to win all the Manx races: 250, 350 and 500cc.

This success is proof of Ron Williams' skill; but what makes it even more outstanding is that the same chassis design was used in all three classes, a rare feat indeed. Credit must also be given to Dugdale's preparation and running of the team.

The list of riders of Maxton machines is almost endless, but at this stage of the company's history it included such names as Chris Mortimer, Tom Herron, John Williams, Charlie Williams, Bernard Murray, Tony Rutter, Steve Parrish, Eddie Roberts, Stan Woods, Roger Marshall and Steve Machin.

At the time, a large percentage of the frames produced

The second chassis for the NR500 engine. This example was built at the Honda works, but under the supervision of Ron Williams.

The complete NR500 racer.

were for Yamaha 125, 250 and 350cc engines. However, frames were also made to take Ducati Pantah V-twins, work that was carried out for Sports Motorcycles, which had Tony Rutter riding for it. Maxton also built frames for CZ, which were raced by Eddie Roberts and Dave Hickman. During the late 1970s, Ron Williams went to work for another major manufacturer when he built a special chassis for Yamaha, to house a three-cylinder, 500cc engine. It was ridden by the Japanese works rider, Takasumi Katayama.

A major advance, which was instrumental in keeping Maxton Engineering among the leading independent frame makers, came about in 1975 when it built its first cantilever machine. This particular chassis housed a 350cc engine, and the machine was an instant success. Ridden by Charlie Williams, it won the Isle of Man Junior TT.

Continued success added to the excellent reputation of Ron Williams and Maxton Engineering, and the company's output included machines for Formula 1. Some of these were based on Suzuki engines, while others used Honda powerplants.

Nineteen-eighty saw the arrival of Maxton's first road bike, though it would be the only one. This one-off, designed and built by Ron Williams himself, used a conventional steel tube chassis and was powered by an RD350 LC Yamaha engine. Also at this time, another new chassis was designed and built, but this one was to change the direction of Ron Williams' career.

Ron had been approached by the research and development department of Honda to build a chassis for the NR500 four-stroke. This engine was the revolutionary oval-piston GP project. On accepting the job, Ron was supplied with a sample engine around which he was to build the chassis. With most new designs, a constructor likes to maintain at least some degree of confidentiality until ready to unveil his work, but with this project Honda insisted that the work be carried out under conditions of utmost secrecy.

When the machine was complete, it was shipped to Honda in Japan, where a full working engine was fitted and a test programme started. Ron Williams' work must have impressed, as he was asked by the team manager of the Honda International Racing Corporation to fly to Japan to assist in the development programme and test work, with the possibility of becoming a consultant to the Honda racing team.

After a visit to the Honda factory, where terms were

A tubular steel frame built around a CZ engine. The finished machine was raced by Dave Hickman and Eddie Roberts.

agreed, Ron became an official consultant to the research and development department. In this new position, he set

about building four more chassis. However, this time all the construction work was carried out by Honda's own employees;

Motorcycle Road & Racing Chassis

A Maxton-built tubular steel chassis for the 1983 MCN Superbike series.

designs showed that Maxton Engineering was keeping up with modern trends. This was his first deltabox design; that is, a twin-spar chassis in which the main members are made from formed aluminium sheet, welded together to form deep box-like sections. This construction, although new in both design and materials, was still made by Maxton in its converted chapel, and three of these aluminium deltabox chassis were made, all to house 250cc engines.

In addition to the alloy frames produced for solo machines, Ron Williams designed and built a sidecar chassis. Again, this was diversification, in two respects. One was that Maxton Engineering had never built a sidecar chassis before; the other was the unfamiliar method of construction, being a stressed-skin aluminium monocoque riveted and glued together. This machine was powered by a Yamaha TZ750 two-stroke.

The 1980s saw Maxton Engineering continue to make technical advances. One notable innovation was achieved in the form of two composite chassis. These machines were designed and built by Ron Williams in his Maxton Engineering factory, and made use of carbon and Kevlar

The swingarm for the Superbike chassis. The finished machine was ridden by Ron Haslam and Wayne Gardner.

Ron was to carry out the design work and then oversee the actual manufacturing process.

So that he could devote sufficient time to this project, Ron scaled down his frame production to a few one-offs that could be built during the closed season. By now, he was travelling the world as a race technician with the Honda GP Team.

During the early 1980s, the closed-season period enabled Ron to carry on designing on his own account. One of these

fibres. Having made his own moulds, Ron used the wet lay-up

Right, top: A cantilever chassis for a 500cc, single-cylinder engine. It was built during 1984.

Right: Maxton took another step forward in 1985, when it introduced its first formed-aluminium, twin-spar frame.

Motorcycle Road & Racing Chassis

A further advance was made by Ron Williams when he produced this carbon fibre composite chassis. The use of this totally different technology demonstrates the innovative thinking behind the company.

Maxton has not restricted its work purely to two-wheeled machines, as this sheet-aluminium sidecar chassis shows.

The rarest of all Maxton machines: the only road bike ever built by the company.

method to produce the laminated chassis members, assembling the two chassis completely in-house.

Originally, the composite chassis were produced to house 250cc Honda and Yamaha engines, but later one was fitted and raced with a 350 Yamaha. Composite technology is vastly different in both design and manufacturing methods to conventional motorcycle frame materials, and these two frames illustrated the skill and versatility of Maxton Engineering.

During the mid-1980s, Ron Williams still managed to produce a small number of tubular steel chassis to take 500 and 600cc four-stroke singles, which by that time constituted a very popular form of racing.

Ron was to make 1987 his last year of working with a Grand Prix team, and this last season was spent with Rothman's International, whose rider was Roger Burnett. In previous years, on the world GP scene with Honda, Ron worked with riders such as Mick Grant, Takasumi Katayama, Wayne Gardner, Roger Marshall, Roger Burnett, Ron Haslam, Joey Dunlop and Richard Scott.

With his globe-trotting days behind him, Ron decided to develop his business again, but not in the manufacture of frames. Instead, he embarked on a completely new venture, building magnesium wheels. With design and development carried out in true Maxton tradition, a three-spoke magnesium wheel went into production in 1988.

During 1989, Ron Williams became aware that there was a strong demand from riders who wanted the means to convert their road bikes for racing, and two areas of motorcycle engineering of particular interest to him were front forks and rear suspension. As a result, a business was built around the conversion and supply of these components, which has led to Maxton Engineering becoming a service centre for Koni, the major manufacturer of suspension components. By 1990, the lure of racing was too much for Ron Williams, so he moved back into the racing business, working for the ill-starred John Player Norton racing team. In 1991, he returned to his great love, designing.

Over the years, Maxton Engineering and Ron Williams have shown great capability and versatility. The list of riders, many of them famous, who have benefited from the skill and dedication shown by Maxton, must be long indeed.

Although Ron Williams and Maxton no longer make motorcycle frames, Maxton is still very much in business and Ron still exercises his skill and vast experience in supplying suspension systems for both racing and road going motorcycles, as well as a valuable service in the re-valving and re-springing of motorcycle forks. Maxton now builds its own shock absorber.

Motorcycle Road & Racing Chassis

A relaxed Ron Williams, the founder of Maxton.

The company will long be remembered for its valuable contribution to the progress of motorcycle frame design, especially by those that have ridden its products. As for Ron Williams, it looks as if his long experience will be put to good use for a while yet.

An example of a shock absorber manufactured in-house at Maxton.

nine

P&M Motorcycles

This well known British manufacturer of racing motorcycle frames used to be known, and will be remembered by some, as Peckett and McNab. That was the original name of the company when it was formed in 1975 by Richard Peckett and Peter McNab.

Richard and Peter met three years prior to forming the company, while working together at Dresda Autos. This employment must have given both of them invaluable experience, which was to be utilized to the full when they began designing

An early example of Peckett and McNab's engineering skills. This frame was built in 1976 to house a BMW flat-twin. It was raced in endurance events by Richard Peckett and Denis McMillan, achieving a sixth place at Zandvoort.

Motorcycle Road & Racing Chassis

A 1979 machine with a 998cc Kawasaki engine. It was designed and built to race in F1 events.

and building motorcycle frames, or modifying existing ones.

Peckett and McNab was formed on capital raised by Richard when he sold his Triumph Trident, which he had built while working at Dresda, and by Peter, who sold his Rob North triple. With the proceeds, they were able to move into premises

P&M built its first road bike in 1980, and this is the first example. The frame held a Kawasaki Z IR engine, bored out to 1100cc, which produced phenomenal performance. Unfortunately, the bike was written off quite early by a P&M employee.

The second road bike utilized many parts salvaged from the original. It is still with its original owner and sees regular use.

A typical P&M chassis being built.

The rising-rate rear suspension arrangement under construction.

in Arragon Street, Twickenham, on 1st November 1975.

In fact, the company's new home was an old builder's yard, but because Richard had had some carpentry experience, and a relative was an electrician, the workshop was soon renovated. The acquisition of some cheap, secondhand machinery saw the company underway.

For a company aiming to manufacture and modify racing motorcycle frames, it had a great asset in that the partners were both motorcyclists. Richard, being a serious race rider, was and still is in a position to know what is required from a new build, and what modifications are required to an existing machine. This knowledge was to prove invaluable over the coming years.

During the early part of the company's existence, almost any engineering jobs were undertaken to get the business going. A Dresda Honda, owned by Richard, was dismantled and the frame was sold. Then, in the evenings when the day's money making work was done, Richard and Peter designed and built a frame to house the Honda engine.

The new machine, which was race prepared for the 1976 season, was their very first, the P&M 1. Unfortunately, on the second lap of the first practice with this machine, the primary chain broke and wrecked the engine. It was rebuilt, and the machine ran on until the end of the season.

That first machine was given a new engine for 1977, and on its first outing, the Transatlantic Meeting at Brands Hatch, it won the four-stroke race and finished eighth in the MCN Superbike race, ridden on both occasions by Richard Peckett himself. More wins followed at club and national events, including a second place at a British Championship meeting. This performance from

One of P&M's last F1 machines, a 750cc, receives attention from its creator, Richard Peckett.

Richard Peckett demonstrating his riding skills on a machine he designed and built. His riding ability has served him well in determining just what is required to get the best from a machine.

its first frame was a very good advertisement for the potential capabilities of the new company.

The second frame built by Peckett and McNab housed a BMW twin, and was ridden in endurance events by Richard Peckett and Denis MacMillan. The last recorded result for this combination of machine and riders was a sixth place at Zandvoort in 1977.

Both partners were still keeping the company going by undertaking any work that came along, but in the evenings, they spent extra hours making jigs and fixtures for producing all the parts that go with a motorcycle frame. All this was in preparation for the production of frames in a professional manner, when the opportunity came their way.

Between other work, frames three and four were designed and built, using a Suzuki 500cc twin and a Kawasaki engine respectively. Richard rode the Kawasaki himself and found that it was very quick, though various engine problems needed attention, however, such as the fitting of an oil cooler, while regular seizing was overcome by fitting a different make of piston. As a matter of interest, this bike would carry on racing for several years, illustrating the soundness of the design and manufacture.

Meanwhile, the partners decided to build a new frame for the original Honda, and Asa Moyse rode the result in the first ever Formula One short-circuit race at Silverstone, while Richard rode the Kawasaki. From the start, Richard held second place to Ron Haslam, but he was soon passed by Alistair Frane. The next few laps saw a close battle with Roger Nichols, but this came to an end when they collided passing a back marker.

The company was taking its racing very seriously, as it was sensibly considered good advertising for its capabilities. To this end, the partners decided to build a new frame for the Kawasaki as well.

An interesting race for Peckett and McNab took place at the last Brands Hatch meeting of 1977. Richard Peckett rode the reframed Kawasaki, Asa Moyse borrowed the old Kawasaki frame, and John Cowie rode the Honda, while the London distributor Mocheck borrowed the old Honda frame. This resulted in the front row of the grid having two works Hondas and four Peckett and McNab machines. The Hondas came first and sixth, while Peckett and McNab bikes were second, third, fourth and fifth. This was an excellent result for the recently-formed company and was, without doubt, responsible for putting it on the map, generating orders for machines for the new F1 series.

Mocheck ordered two bikes, and Jim Wells and Tony Osborne one each, while more orders came in from other riders. This got the 1978 season off to an excellent start, and to add to its racing commitment, an agreement was made to supply a chassis for John Cowie and Bernie Toleman to ride in endurance races. The engine and running expenses for this were to be provided by Albion Street Motors, in whose colours the machine would run.

The first meeting for the endurance machine was at Le Mans, where it finished a very creditable third. This excellent placing at an important venue drew attention to the machine, and an offer of help came from Girling, whose rear shock absorbers were being used. At this point, the agreement with Albion Street Motors came to an early end, and the machine ran in the Peckett and McNab red and white colour scheme for the rest of the season.

P&M was kept busy, as John Cowie wanted to compete in the new F1 series as well as in endurance racing, and the partners were constantly changing the machine from one spec to the other. As well as supplying Steve Manship with an F1 Kawasaki, the company also ran a third machine for Richard Peckett himself. However, 1978 was not a good riding season for Richard. He suffered a broken shoulder blade at the beginning of the season, and never seemed to get it together after that. Almost certainly, his workload prevented him from giving his riding its usual effort.

Despite Richard's problems, 1978 was a very good year for the company, both from the amount of business transacted and results from company-supported machinery. The highlight was John Cowie winning the F1 Championship, while another high point was his win at Silverstone, beating Tom Herron and Mike Hailwood in the process.

The Silverstone victory was not without some drama, as John Cowie's machine was a candidate for disqualification. At the time, the rules stated that all engines must use standard carburettors and that no major welding was allowed to crankcases. As the Peckett and McNab machine also served as an endurance racer, the oil filler aperture in the crankcase had been machined to accept a large-bore alloy tube, which had been welded in with an adaptor to prevent oil from contaminating the clutch. This gave no technical advantage whatsoever, and only served to assist filling during endurance events. In the F1 race, the fuel and oil were put in prior to the race. Moreover, it was pointed out that the crankcases of Mike Hailwood's machine had considerable welding modifications to fit certain parts.

In addition to the modified crankcase, P&M's machine was also claimed to have bored-out carburettors, the bore being measured at 28.5mm instead of the regulation 28mm. It was pointed out to the scrutineer that the carburettors were as purchased with the engine. Some brand-new carburettors were located and measured; they, too, were 28.5mm. Then it was discovered that they were being measured in the wrong place. Measured correctly, they were of the required 28mm bore, so John Cowie was the confirmed winner.

Honda borrowed a Peckett and McNab chassis for Ron Haslam to ride in the last F1 meeting of the season, at Brands Hatch. In winning the race, he set a lap record that was to stand for several seasons. This was excellent testimony to the abilities of the company as a motorcycle chassis builder.

As well as the excellent performance from Peckett and McNab machines during this first season of the new F1 series, the company's bikes produced some notable performances in endurance racing, including a third at Le Mans, a fourth at Spa, twelfth at the Bol d'Or, and sixth and seventh places at Brands Hatch. Among a series of good performances, there are usually times when things don't go to plan, and Peckett and McNab were no exceptions to this rule. The P&M machine suffered a crash at the Nürburgring, and an engine seizure in Barcelona.

Due to the engine seizure, some hurried work was put in at P&M to rebuild the engine for the Race of Aces meeting at Snetterton that coming weekend. This rebuild was completed on the Saturday afternoon, and the engine put into the bike to leave for Snetterton that very evening. However, it still needed running in, so an unnamed member of the crew stopped the transporter at about midnight, removed the bike from the back and, using the endurance lights, rode it the last 60 miles to Snetterton!

All this effort proved justified, for despite falling from a 125cc Honda in an earlier race and being badly bruised, John Cowie went on to win the race for Peckett and McNab from Phil Read. This type of performance was surely not going unnoticed, and by this time, Dunlop was supplying the team with tyres of the same specification as those supplied to the top riders.

If there was any doubt that P&M was widely respected in motorcycle racing, it was dismissed in the winter of 1978-79, when Honda asked if it would be interested in running Honda-powered bikes for the 1979 season. The deal was that P&M would receive help from Gilberts of Catford, and Honda would loan three race-prepared engines. These were to be based on the CB900 that was due out at that time. The offer was accepted, two machines being built for Roger Marshall and Tony Rutter. Honda also ordered a rolling chassis for its works team. As it turned out, the chassis supplied to Honda Britain from Japan were good, so the P&M frame was not used.

A Peckett and McNab machine was ridden during the season by Alex George, who achieved some good results. Normally, this machine would have been ridden by Richard Peckett himself, but he was taking a sabbatical to get married. During this period, Peter McNab looked after the racing side of the business.

At the end of 1979, Peter announced that he wanted to leave P&M. Richard Peckett was prepared to purchase his share and, by the following October, they had parted company. Richard decided to rename the company P&M Motorcycles, as

Left-side view of the current P&M classic racer, the Trident.

by now the machines had become known as P&Ms, so the new abbreviated title seemed appropriate.

Peter McNab didn't get away from P&Ms completely, however, as a gentleman by the name of George Beale bought two of them. Peter went to work for his team, running the two machines for riders Roger Marshall and Graham Macgregor.

During 1980, P&M was to take a step in another direction,

Right-side view of the Trident.

This fine action shot shows Richard Peckett racing his Trident in one of the popular classic events.

to produce a road bike. This used a secondhand ZIR Kawasaki power unit, bored out to 1100cc, and was road-tested by most of the leading motorcycle magazines, which in all cases, were full of praise for the first road-going P&M. In fact, one magazine was very reluctant to return the machine after testing.

Its performance was pretty shattering, covering the standing quarter-mile in 11 seconds, and with a maximum speed approaching 150mph. Despite this performance, it would still average 40-45mpg on a run. But just when P&M had found a winner from a business point of view, disaster struck. Out on the road, one of their employees crashed into a Rover, writing off the new bike. Fortunately, the rider lived to tell the tale.

Richard Peckett bought the wreck from the insurance company and, using the recoverable parts, built another road bike. Again, it found favour with the motorcycle magazines, and was soon purchased by a customer, who traded-in his P&M racer in part exchange. The same owner kept the bike for several years.

P&M took another step forward in 1981 when it produced its first monoshock chassis for Jim Wells to race. As usual with a new design, several chassis of this type were sold to customers wishing to have the latest P&M machines. But despite the successes, this was a difficult period for P&M, as the buyout had left Richard Peckett short of development money, and, as competitors began to catch up technically, sales began to drop off.

Although P&M was unable to introduce completely new innovations every year, it did make continual improvements to its chassis to improve performance. It also tried to make changes that could be utilized by the owners of older P&M chassis. Considering past customers in this way was a great credit to the company. During this time, many customers who sold their P&M racers in favour of other makes were disappointed by their new machines, and soon returned to P&M for another chassis that was more to their liking.

In 1983 Richard Peckett designed and built a rising-rate rocker arm frame for Jim Wells to race in F1. In addition, P&M

The man in charge, Richard Peckett.

built a monoshock frame for F2 racing, using a 550cc Kawasaki, bored out to 600cc. Jim Wells also rode this machine.

P&M suffered more interruptions to its normal smooth running in 1984. First it lost its star riders when Jim Wells left with Asa Moyse. Both were to ride Harris-made machines in the new F1 750 series, and it was a sponsored deal which P&M could not match, and the two riders could not ignore. To add to this, the lease on the factory came to an end and could not be renewed, forcing a move to modern premises, which were purchased.

A production Trident nearing completion.

Three P&M Tridents wait to do battle. Richard Peckett's works machine is in the foreground.

During 1985, P&M extended its technical expertise even further when it designed a frame that had an adjustable head angle. This could be changed from 62 degrees to 64 degrees in ½ degree increments, and the change could be carried out in two or three minutes.

On a competitive machine, this innovation could be a race-winning asset. A test by Alan Cathcart, whose opinion is rated highly, raved about this machine, although its ageing 750cc air-cooled Kawasaki engine was no match for the new four-valve Suzuki. Without the power to win, the new design was destined not to have the opportunity it deserved, a familiar story for smaller manufacturers with good designs, not having the resources to develop their innovations.

The following year, 1986, P&M designed and built a monoshock chassis for the new GPZ Kawasaki engine. With this chassis, and an engine prepared by Mistral Engineering, Ray Swann won the British F2 championship. But by the late 1980s, the sale of new P&M frames had almost ceased. The reduction in demand for special frames was due to the general improvement in factory frames. It applied to a lesser extent to road bikes, but these became one-offs or limited editions, which made manufacture and marketing expensive.

However, P&M had too much experience to let it go to waste, and the company found a new outlet in the boom in classic racing. Having built and raced a Trident, Richard Peckett had invaluable experience in this area, and as the three-cylinder Triumph was very popular with classic racers, P&M soon found a workable business in producing replicas of his original frame.

Richard built up two Tridents that he raced himself, while Phil Godfrey had another two, raced for him by Phil Davenport, and the business went on to produce more replicas. Although the demand for special racing frames from P&M had almost ceased by the late 1980s, the company still holds and maintains all the necessary spares to service the many P&M machines still racing in a variety of club and other events.

From the very beginning, the success of P&M designs speaks for itself, but the build quality matches the design, only the very best materials having been used. Frames are manufactured from T45 or Reynolds 531 tubing in 17 and 18swg. All are nickel-bronze welded. Fork yokes are fabricated steel, bronze welded with different offsets to facilitate the adjustment of trail. These yokes are also produced with standard bores. Head bearings are sealed taper-roller, and to ensure accuracy P&M now finish-bores the head stock after removal from the welding jig. Swingarms are fabricated from box-section material, with a pressing running down its length to give greater stiffness, and use sealed taper-roller bearings.

All the P&M frames of the period followed a set specification:

Wheelbase:	145-147cm
Trail:	10-13cm
Head angle:	62 degrees
Weight:	181kg
Forks:	35mm Ceriani
Discs:	2 x 25cm front; 1 x 23cm rear
Calipers/master cylinders:	Lockheed
Wheels:	CMA five-spoke
Engines:	Kawasak (100bhp at rear wheel) or Honda (105bhp at rear wheel)

Changes to the original specification, in later years, included the use of 38mm Ceriani and Marzocchi forks, Dymag and Astralite wheels, and Spondon discs and four-pot Lockheed calipers. On the frame side, the head angle was changed to 63 degrees, while the wheelbase was shortened to 143.5cm, then 141cm.

A collection of P&M machines at a Snetterton race meeting.

Motorcycle Road & Racing Chassis

Go it alone?

It is evident that P&M Motorcycles has established a reputation as a producer of very competitive and successful racing motorcycle frames. Its results in F1, F2 and endurance racing confirm this. One major factor in this success story is that Richard Peckett also raced the machines he designed and built. This provided essential feedback of the information needed to get the best from a machine.

The handling of P&M frames has always been highly rated, and they have a reputation for being well built. This latter point is borne out by the fact that over 100 frames have been built since the formation of the company in 1975, and, as far as is known, only one has been destroyed – the first road bike by that P&M employee who ran into a Rover. A large percentage of the others are still putting in racing miles, and are sought after by enthusiasts.

All this sprang from two men who began in a tiny workshop, and extra credit is due when you realize that, in the very beginning, all the tubes used in the frames were bent by hand. This changed, of course, when the business became established and a purpose-built hydraulic bending machine was finally purchased.

Although P&M's success centred on frame design and construction, it must be mentioned that some of the company's own racing successes were due to the engine building talents of Richard Peckett. He had the ability to squeeze extra performance from factory engines, without sacrificing reliability.

As time passes, trends in motorcycle racing change, the formula formats are revised, and engine sizes altered, while the competitive nature of the sport leads to technical advances. The major factory-produced machines are improved to make the over-the counter racer more competitive, which is one reason why the demand for specially-built frames from the independent manufacturers has dropped off. Although there will always be independent chassis manufacturers and a market for their products, it would appear that they have to be more specialized. P&M has recognized this, and has responded to the commercial needs of business by exploiting the now-popular classic bike racing.

It's interesting to speculate on what the company may produce in the future. Perhaps a new racing formula will open the door again, or possibly P&M may accept the expense and administration requirements of marketing a road machine. Whatever it chooses to design and manufacture, motorcycling enthusiasts will benefit from machines admired by many.

Machines built by P&M continue to have a keen following and with the ever growing interest in classic bikes, its great experience enables P&M to give excellent service in most areas to meet the needs of the ever growing band of classic bike enthusiasts.

P&M continues to produce frames where required, which includes re-framing machines that are just tired, and those that are damaged in crashes. Richard Peckett continues to use his well known engine building skills, and is still continuing development of the three-cylinder Trident engine.

Along with R J Quaife Engineering, the company has produced a six-speed gearbox for the Trident, to complement the belt drive transmission previously produced. Another development from P&M is a new larger capacity oil pump to cater for the use of modern synthetic oils, which Richard Peckett is now in favour of to replace the castor-based oils that were previously used. There are two versions of the new pump from P&M. The first one produces a 50 per cent increase in flow over the old Triumph pump, and is proving to be ideal for relatively low-revving road machines. For race engines, another version produces a 21 per cent increase in flow whilst retaining the required return levels.

Another serious Trident problem taken in hand by P&M is the breaking of cylinder barrels. To overcome this, a new casting was developed, thicker and cast from a modern alloy which, when heat treated, gives greater strength. The increase in strength has allowed engines of larger bore to be produced. One version using a P&M crank with 7mm longer stroke in conjunction with 3mm shorter con rods results in a 930cc engine, which in racing trim produces 100bhp – standard 750cc engines produce 58bhp. P&M will make engine parts that are no longer available in an effort to keep Trident engines running as long as the enthusiasts require them.

Apart from its frame making skills, P&M produces high-performance front forks. These utilise aluminium sliders for road going machines and magnesium ones for racing.

P&M Motorcycles has always had the technical bonus that Richard Peckett has been a serious motorcycle racer for most of his adult life. This experience is invaluable when designing and building race bikes. Richard still races, although a bad crash at Snetterton in 1995 resulted in a bad injury to his right shoulder, so he now rides at selected meetings.

P&M is likely to keep busy thanks to the new class in classic racing for post classics, allowing for the use of machines made up to December 1986. P&M prepared machines, such as the Kawasaki Z900, the Suzuki GS1000 and the Honda CB750 and CB900, which were produced in 1976 for the F1 series, will again see serious racing, and further developments on this front are possible.

P&M Motorcycles has given a great deal to the development of motorcycles in the areas in which it specialises, and will continue to do so.

ten

PDQ

Not all the people with the ability to build motorcycle frames actually turn their skills into a big business. However, one person who has made a significant contribution to frame-making technology, while continuing to run a normal motorcycle sales and preparation business, is Larry Webb, the proprietor of PDQ.

Larry began his association with motorcycles by working in various retailers' workshops, where he gained valuable mechanical experience. As his knowledge grew, so did the desire to do this type of work for himself, in his own business. During 1977, while working for Motor Racing Enterprises on racing cars, he finally decided to make the break and work for himself. His late employer rented him a workshop at the rear of its premises, and Larry was in business.

The first title Larry used for his enterprise was LDM, and his new venture catered for those who required machines prepared for racing, or who wanted modifications to frames, to improve structural performance.

Spending time on race frame modification led eventually to the design and construction of his first complete motorcycle frame, and this was built from round-section steel tubing, to accommodate an H2R Kawasaki 750cc engine.

Larry Webb aboard the first machine he designed and built.

Motorcycle Road & Racing Chassis

A pair of stunt bikes strengthened and prepared by Larry Webb for Eddy Kidd.

The completed machine was notable in one respect, and that was its size. Although the frame held a 750cc engine, the bike's overall size was similar to that of a 250 racer. Larry also claims that this frame was the first ever to boast fully-floating rear suspension, which he conceived to solve a problem half-way through construction, rather than it being an integral part of the design from the beginning.

Larry built the machine as a one-off, for his personal use, and raced it in UK clubman events for two seasons. There were no great results but he later said that his novice status as a rider may have been part of the reason.

During this period, the main income for LDM still came from modification work and rebuilds. Then an opportunity arose for him to go back to working on race cars for Johnny Dumfries, which was too tempting to pass up, so LDM ceased trading. However, Larry had not forgotten bikes, or single-cylinder engines, partly because he spent some time working on go-karts. Then

he received, and accepted, an offer to work for Eddy Kidd, the world-famous stunt rider, which meant working on motorcycle frames again.

Larry was required to strengthen frames to cope with the landing loads from the record-breaking jumps made by Eddy Kidd. This was in addition to the general preparation and maintenance of all the machines used in the stunts. At the end of a two-year stint, however, he went back to working on cars again, until the firm that employed him folded – it was time to get back into business on his own account.

That was how PDQ was formed in 1984, as a general motorcycle workshop, catering for rebuilds, modifications, and the retail of motorcycles, spares and accessories. However, Larry Webb was to become involved in the construction of another interesting design. During the late 1980s, in conjunction with Norman Hossack, he built a machine that had a unique front suspension layout.

The Yamaha V-Max converted by PDQ to single-leg rear suspension, while retaining the shaft drive. This is a standard conversion offered by the company.

This frame was built by PDQ to compete in drag racing. It makes use of a large-section spine, but retains the down tubes of the original bike to comply with the relevant class regulations.

vertical members which, in effect, replaced the normal fork legs. These were mounted to the frame by means of a pair of wishbones, the lower one operating the cantilever-mounted single damper unit. Steering was taken care of by rotation of the whole upright in a bearing head that replaced the original head.

The Norman Hossack design was for a wishbone-type front suspension. This was based on rigid, rectangular-section steel

Motorcycle Road & Racing Chassis

In order to develop this suspension, the front end was removed from Larry's Kawasaki GPZ 1100B1 frame, and the new front welded on. The rear suspension utilized the original Kawasaki swingarm, with additional bracing welded on to enhance stiffness.

This design of front suspension was claimed to be more rigid than conventional forks, while the steering geometry remained more constant during braking and cornering. As an added bonus, it was also claimed to have improved suspension response.

At the time Larry Webb carried out this conversion to his personal Kawasaki, it was agreed that PDQ would perfect the system for road use and convert customers' machines, while Norman Hossack would cater for the race versions. However, for the usual commercial reasons, PDQ did not pursue the project.

Norman Hossack continued to carry out the conversion for both road and race use, and various large-engined Japanese machines would receive the treatment, along with a few BMWs and a Laverda. PDQ, meanwhile, made a wide variety of modifications to road machines, one of which did become popular – the conversion of the Yamaha V-Max to single-leg rear suspension, while retaining its shaft drive.

During 1990, PDQ built another rather special frame, this one for drag racing, using a Suzuki GT750 engine. It was an interesting project, as, in order to comply with the class regulations, the lower frame tubes from the original factory frame had to be retained.

The frame was based on a large, deep-section spine, which was fabricated from steel. The remainder of the frame was constructed from round-section steel tubing, and included the obligatory tubes from the original frame. Suitable front forks and rear swingarm completed this special-purpose frame, which was successful, taking several wins in its class.

Move to suspension

During the 1990s PDQ slowly drifted away from producing frames or complete machines, but was kept busy with the development and manufacture of motorcycle suspensions.

Although PDQ may not have been the most prolific frame maker to date, Larry Webb's claim to be the first to produce fully-floating rear suspension, his involvement in the wishbone front suspension, and his endless frame modifications, are all contributions to the advancement of motorcycle frame technology.

A PDQ Battlemax prototype, 1994. (Courtesy Roland Brown)

eleven

Quasar

A motorcycle that the rider sits in, rather than on, with feet forward, and under a roof, must be considered if not unique, then at least very different. The Quasar was just such a design.

Quasar was the brainchild of Malcolm Newell, a keen English motorcyclist. 'Keen' is almost an understatement in describing Malcolm as in his life he owned over 140 motorcycles. He began his commercial career in motorcycling by managing a bike dealership, which eventually led to him running his own shop.

Even though the shop was his own business, Malcolm eventually decided that retailing was not as rewarding as construction, so the shop was replaced by a workshop. This decision was taken during the 1960s and early 1970s, and led to a few one-off bikes and trikes being designed and built. During the course of his work, Malcolm met Ken Leaman, an engineer who agreed with him that the idea of a motorcycle that was sat in, rather than on, appeared to offer many advantages. These included a lower centre of gravity and improved aerodynamics, and the result of their collaboration was a prototype – the Probe – which would become the Quasar.

The Mk I Quasar had a tubular steel frame, which housed an in-line, four-cylinder, 850cc Reliant engine. It retained the Reliant transmission, which had synchromesh on all four gears and shaft-drive to the rear wheel. The front suspension and steering were by a leading-link system, while the rear featured a swingarm.

The bodywork was of fibreglass and incorporated a windscreen and full roof, an arrangement which offered improved aerodynamics over a conventional motorcycle, and gave the rider much better weather protection than that provided by a conventional bike. The pillion passenger shared the same creature comforts. The machine's long wheelbase (2007mm), coupled with the low riding position, resulted in excellent stability, especially during cornering, and the result was a fast and comfortable machine which handled well. Without sufficient capital and engineering facilities, Newell and Leaman handed over the project to a company called Wilson and Sons, which produced the first pre-production machines, followed by ten production bikes, the first sold in 1976.

By 1980, Wilson and Sons had handed the project to another company which became known as Quasar Motorcycles Ltd. This company had a contract to build five machines, and two were displayed at that year's Earls Court Show. A version built to be evaluated by the Avon and Somerset, Wiltshire and Lancashire Police Forces was shown on the Cibie stand. The remaining three bikes ordered were sold in early 1981, which marked the end of the Quasar Mk I.

While all this was going on, Malcolm Newell had set about producing a hub-centre steering system, based on a Bob Tait patent. To raise the necessary capital, he produced some feet-forward machines called Phasers. One version was exhibited

Motorcycle Road & Racing Chassis

common units were the Suzuki GS850 and 1000.

By 1987 Malcolm Newell had built the first rear-engined sports Quasar. This was hub-centred steered, had a GPZ1100 engine and was expected to be capable of exceeding 200mph.

The Mk II Quasar, with an even lower centre of gravity than its predecessor, and the suspension advantages associated with hub-centre steering, produced exciting performance and handling potential. This was complemented by very-low-drag bodywork that was roofless. The result was a machine that offered very high speed with handling to match. The Mk II Quasar did reach production, and could be purchased in kit form, not restricted to any specific engine – over ten were sold.

In the 1990s Malcolm was still building Mk II Quasars, mainly around the Suzuki GS1000 engine. Also during the early 1990s a second rear-engined Sports Quasar was well underway, but this time using Kawasaki's Z1300 six.

In 1992 Malcolm Newell announced his latest creation, which he referred to as Quasar Mk III, but it was an entirely new invention and, therefore, a concept vehicle. And 'vehicle' was a safe description, as it could have three or more wheels.

Despite having more than two wheels, Quasar Mk III was a banking vehicle, just like a motorcycle. Each pair of wheels (on the same axle line) was interconnected by means of a mechanical rocking arm, or an hydraulic, electrical or pneumatic equivalent. This arrangement enabled the interconnected wheels to maintain a relatively equal contact pressure with the ground while the vehicle banked. The rocking arm, or equivalent, could be locked in any position by means of a disc brake and caliper (or other system), which prevented the vehicle from banking and could hold it in a vertical position without the operator having to balance it. The rocking arm, or its equivalent, always remained parallel to the ground, which enabled the fitting of aerodynamic control surfaces, which would remain parallel to the ground while the vehicle banked.

at the 1981 NEC Motorcycle Show, using hub-centre steering and a Kawasaki Z1300 engine. Another version of this machine was was tested by *Motorcycle Weekly* magazine, showing a top speed of 160.1mph.

The following year saw the formation of Design Revolution by Malcolm Newell and Bob Tait, to build hub-centre steered successors to the original Quasar. Two models were proposed, the 'Kymera' using a Honda Gold Wing engine, and the 'Dragoon' with Moto Guzzi mechanics. These and all of Malcolm's later heavyweight machines used the hub-centre steering system designed by Bob Tait. In the end, six were built with Gold Wing engines and several more using the Moto Guzzi V-twin. There were also some lightweight versions built with Yamaha 250 and 350LC engines.

By 1984, Malcolm was again concentrating on the design and construction of Quasars, resulting in the Mk II. The Mk II was based on the same concept as the original Quasar, but differed from the Mk I in several ways, there being some significant technical changes. Although the frame was of similar layout and retained the sit-in/feet-forward riding position, it employed hub-centre steering, while the choice of engine differed. Japanese, multi-cylinder engines were used, mounted across the frame – the Reliant had been mounted in-line with the frame – and the first bike used a Kawasaki Z1300 six-cylinder unit, though the most

The Quasar presented at the 1975 Earls Court Show used Reynolds 531 tubing; the frame had rectangular section pivoted forks at both ends with Girling gas-filled shocks. As Vic Willoughby pointed out in *The Motor Cycle*, 'Ticking over in Malcolm Newell's mind are thoughts of hub-centre steering'. (Courtesy EMAP)

In today's increasingly heavy traffic, the motorcycle provides the most time- and space-effective means of transporting one or two people. However, where safety and comfort are concerned, it is greatly inferior to the car. To provide adequate levels of safety, the occupants of cars must be restrained within a rigid shell, capable of withstanding a major impact. It is not possible to provide this with a conventional motorcycle. Malcolm Newell's Quasar Mk III promised to be a narrow-tracked vehicle in which the occupants would be fully enclosed by a rigid shell that does not have to be balanced while stationary.

The method of interlinking the wheels in the basic design could have been achieved in a number of ways. In one case, a leaf spring would provide both the interlinking connection and shock absorption; in another, the interlinking rocker arm connected to dampers with coil springs. The latter arrangement would have allowed the suspension and rocker arm to be replaced by electrical, hydraulic or pneumatic linkages.

In each case, as the vehicle banked, all wheels would remain in contact with the ground; this ensured by a centrally-mounted pivot for the rocking arm, leaf spring, etc. The mechanism of support provided a parallelogram of linkages. The upper and lower swingarms were pivoted from four points attached to either the front or rear bulkhead, or both. The arms extended backwards, or forwards, of the pivot points, and connected with the two kingpin posts. They were free to rotate only in a vertical plane. Thus, one wheel was free to move in a vertical plane, independently of the other, but within the constraint of the available suspension movement.

It is sad to relate that the exciting and innovative machine just described was not to be completed, as on the 16th April 1994 Malcolm Newell died of a heart attack, at the young age of 54.

Although Malcolm is sadly not going to further the development of his unique designs, what he achieved is significant in the terms of motorcycle design and warrants his place among those that have helped motorcycle progress. Today, looking at the profusion of feet-forward scooters, the roofed BMW C1 and Piaggio's banking three-wheeled MP-3, it's easy to see that Malcolm Newell was ahead of his time.

twelve

Rickman

During the 1960s and 1970s, the name Rickman needed no introduction to European motorcycling enthusiasts. The company's fine reputation began with the design and production of motocross frames, although at that time the sport was known as scrambling. Road racing frames followed, as did road-legal motorcycles.

The company was formed by two brothers, Derek and Don Rickman, both of whom had been successful scrambles riders. Derek began competing on BSAs during 1950, while Don followed two years later, also on a BSA. Their competition careers were to prove invaluable when they began to build scrambles frames, as they had first-hand knowledge of what was required from that type of machine. Moreover, they had gained many contacts in the motorcycle industry.

In 1958 the Rickman brothers opened a retail motorcycle shop in New Milton, in the south of England. By that time, they had also decided that they wanted to build their own scramblers, and, with the help of Tiny Camfield, of road racing fame, they began to build a machine for Derek. This first Rickman consisted of a Triumph T100 engine mounted in a modified BSA frame, with a BSA gearbox and Norton forks. A similar machine was built for Don.

Metisse was the name given to the Rickman machines from the very beginning, and it continued to be used until the company

Derek Rickman scrambling a Metisse MkIII fitted with a Matchless engine.

The production Rickman Bultaco Metisse.

stopped building bikes. There is an interesting story behind the use of this name. The first Rickman machine was built using major components from several different factory machines and, therefore, was very much a hybrid. Since the French for hybrid, 'metisse', sounded right, it was chosen as the name that would be applied to all Rickman frames.

During 1960, a MkII Metisse was produced. Again, this utilized a modified BSA frame, but it differed from the MkI in its use of fibreglass components. Doug Mitchenal, of Avon Fairings, had put forward the idea that fibreglass could be used to great advantage, and the result was that the MkII Metisse sported a combined seat and tail unit, which incorporated the air filter, oil tank, and plates for the competition numbers. This unit was actually bonded to the BSA frame, and, at the time, it was quite an innovative feature, bound to attract attention.

The first Rickman-designed and built frame appeared in 1961, and it became the Metisse MkIII. It was constructed from 1¼in diameter Reynolds 531 tubing with a 16swg wall thickness. Ken Sprayson, technical engineer of the Reynolds Tube Company, was of considerable assistance

To prove that both Rickman brothers were serious competitors, here is Don aboard a Metisse powered by a Bultaco engine.

One of three identical motocross machines campaigned by the Rickman brothers and Eddie Burroughs. The engine is the G85 CS 500cc Matchless. These machines were built with future production in mind; note the distinctive fibreglass panels.

quality was to become a feature of Rickman products.

A prototype batch of three identical MkIII Metisse frames was built to house 500cc Matchless engines, their fibreglass parts were all finished in the very distinctive British Racing Green.

At this time, the frames were being built purely for the personal use of the Rickman brothers, the extra machine being for Eddie Burroughs, who had joined the business. However, they were also built with future production in mind, which was one of the reasons for the use of the Matchless engine. Matchless was prepared to supply Rickman with engine and gearbox units directly from the factory, whereas Triumph was not.

In many ways, the Matchless engine was ideal, particularly for scrambling. It was strong, tunable, and comparatively easy to maintain, and it turned out to be a very wise choice for the Metisse.

The Rickman brothers, being very accomplished

during the development of this frame, as was the Siff Bronze Company, which gave invaluable help with the bronze welding technique used. This excellent form of welding was utilized on all subsequent Rickman frames, and such attention to detail and

The engine mounting details of a MkIII Metisse frame, built for a Triumph engine with separate gearbox. Note the cut-away to show the filter arrangement.

This late 1960s photograph shows the MkIV Metisse frame. It differed from the previous model by having head and downtubes with a greater sweep-back. The engine is a BSA B40 Victor.

It is not surprising that motocross machines were an important part of the company's work, given that both of the Rickman brothers were competitors.

Motorcycle Road & Racing Chassis

A Metisse road racing frame for a non-unit Triumph twin. In the finished machine, the engine was faired in.

An example of the first road racing frame designed and built by Rickman. This early version could accommodate the Matchless G45 or G50 engine. In the hands of Bill Ivy, the prototype won its very first race at a British National Championship meeting during 1966.

scrambles riders, were the ideal marketing tool for the new machine, and their successes soon drew attention to the Metisse, which led to requests for replica kits. In a very short time, orders began to flood in, not only from the UK, but also from Europe and, a little later, from America and Australia.

The MkIII frame was soon adapted to accept the Triumph engine, and over the next few years the Metisse became one of the most popular scrambles machines available. An example of this popularity was that at the 1964 Moto Cross de Nations, at Hawkstone, when over half the riders were Metisse-mounted.

During this early successful period, many famous riders were to take advantage of the Rickman frame, including Nic Jansen and Hubert Scaillet from Belgium, Andy Lee and Ivor England from England, and Sten Lundin from Sweden. American film stars Steve McQueen and Clint Walker were also Metisse fans. The business potential from the USA was sufficient for an agent to be appointed, which resulted in many frame kits being sold there.

During 1964, production of Metisse frames had outgrown the workshop at the back of the Rickmans' retail shop, and as

The CR (Café Racer) Metisse, a road-going version of the race frame. This example has a Triumph engine and was supplied to the famous rider, Giacomo Agostini.

the future looked excellent, new factory premises were acquired in New Milton. More staff were employed, some of whom were also competitive riders. This speaks highly of the esteem in which the Rickman name was held, and it was at this time that Herbert Evemy (a school friend) joined the company as a director.

During the latter part of 1965, a prototype MkIV Metisse was built. This model had a different frame layout, the head and down tubes being swept back more. The new frame was originally built to accommodate the Triumph T100 engine, which was of unit construction, and later, the BSA B40 Victor engine was also fitted. In addition to the new frame layout, all the fibreglass panels were redesigned, the styling being sharpened to create a new look.

Earlier, in 1963, the Rickman brothers had gone to Spain to develop a motocross machine for the Bultaco factory. When they returned, they brought with them a 200cc Bultaco engine, and this was fitted into a much-modified MkIII Metisse frame. One major modification to the frame was that it had a single front downtube in place of the normal twin downtubes. This machine was known as the Petite Metisse, and it was the first two-stroke machine ever built by Rickman.

The two-stroke Metisse proved popular, and a few years later, when Bultaco produced a 250cc engine, Rickman designed a completely new frame to accommodate it. Modified versions of the MkIV fibreglass panels were used. This particular model was the first complete motorcycle that the Rickman brothers offered

An early Triumph-engined CR Metisse. Note the disc brake, a very advanced feature for the 1960s.

A later version of the Triumph CR Metisse.

on the UK market, and over 500 were sold. Bultaco produced an identical model, which was sold worldwide, although mainly in the USA.

A dramatic change was to occur at Rickman in 1966. Until then, its designs were mainly for motocross and some street-legal machines. However, an approach was made by Tim Kirby and BP's racing manager, who asked Rickman to look at the possibility of designing and building a road racing frame.

Metisse CR 750 four-cylinder.

Motorcycle Road & Racing Chassis

A version of the Zundapp-engined Metisse built for the British SAS.

Rickman rose to the occasion, producing a frame that was an immediate success in every sense of the word. Ridden by Bill Ivy, it won first time out at a British National Championship meeting at Mallory Park. This first model could accommodate Matchless G45 and G50 engines.

Success in road racing led to a demand for replicas, so it was put into full production. The frame was built to house a variety of engines, including Triumph's 500 and 650cc twins and the 750cc Norton as well as the Matchless singles. A modified version of this frame was built to house an Italian Aermacchi engine, while other engines used were the Weslake road racing engine and, a few years later, the Helmut Fath four-cylinder unit. One interesting point about the road racing frame is that it was fitted with one of the first disc brakes used on a motorcycle.

The success of this Rickman frame caught the attention of a British police force, for whom the company built a model based on a slightly modified road race frame. This housed a

Triumph engine and was fitted with fibreglass bodywork tailored specifcally for police use.

Rickman modified the police type frame and used it to produce a street-legal motorcycle. Initially, it was fitted with the Triumph engine, but later in 1974, was altered so that four-cylinder Honda, Suzuki and Kawasaki engines could be fitted. This model was designated CR, short for café racer. Later, the frame received further slight modifications, and was fitted with a one-piece fairing and body unit, it became the Rickman Endurance.

All of these new bikes sold in considerable numbers, but fortunately, Rickman was quite capable of coping with volume production, having made yet another move to a much larger factory in 1969, in order to build more 125 and 250cc machines for the American market.

The 125 used a Zundapp engine and was produced as both a motocross version and a street-legal Enduro. The 250 was Montessa-powered and offered in motocross form

Rickman found a big market in the USA for small-capacity motocross machines. Here a Metisse frame houses a 125cc Zundapp engine.

only. Production of these machines rose to 72 per week, and over a three-year period many thousands were shipped to the USA. The Zundapp-engined Enduro was developed for rural police use, being sold to forces throughout the UK during the early 1970s. Later, a similar model was developed for the SAS.

One famous rider to start his career on a Rickman Zundapp 125 was Graham Noyce, who rode one in schoolboy events. Later, he joined Rickman as an apprentice toolmaker, but went on to ride the factory 125s and 250s. During 1973, a special-framed 400cc Husqvarna was built for Graham, on which he won many races before he was signed up for the Maico factory.

Another commercial venture for Rickman during the early 1970s came about when 130 Royal Enfield 750cc twin-cylinder engines were offered to the factory. Once again, the ever-faithful, street-legal Metisse frame was called upon, being modified to accept the Enfield engine. The result was a batch of complete road-going machines.

But during the 1970s, Rickman was to experience at first hand the effect of the stranglehold the Japanese were beginning to gain on the market. Japanese competition machines were cheaper, due to the huge backing of the factories. This led to rapid development, which soon began to eclipse the more expensive Rickmans. Unfortunately, much the same happened to the road-going machines. The early Japanese road bikes might have had poor handling, but they were powered by superb engines, and again, with their immense resources, the Japanese soon began to produce frames to match the engines, which left little room in the market for the Rickman frames. One wonders

if any Rickman creations – or for that matter Harris, or Bakker, or any of the other machines featured in this book – were ever stripped down under an appraising oriental eye ...

As a result of the diminishing market, 1980 saw the Rickman brothers reluctantly give up the design and manufacture of motorcycle frames. They went on to produce motorcycle accessories, such as fairings, safety bars, carriers, and a range of luggage and helmet boxes. But by 2007, you could once again buy a new Metisse frame. Metisse motorcycles offered a complete range, including a MkIII frame kit suitable for Pre-65 Motocross, and the Petite frame for Bultaco engines, as well as flat-track and trail-style frames. So the Rickman brothers' work lives on.

Distinguished service

The Rickman brothers made a significant contribution to the development of motorcycle frames, having dominated the scrambles/motocross market, and then produced successful road racing frames and street-legal machines. No book on independent motorcycle frame makers would be complete without a record of their contribution.

thirteen

Colin Seeley Racing

Long before Colin Seeley became renowned for the design and manufacture of racing motorcycles, he had enjoyed a very successful career as a racing sidecar rider. During 1960 Colin was riding solo scrambles and began to race sidecar outfits in road racing. Towards the end of that year, he bought a G50 Matchless and modified it to accept a sidecar. With this machine his sidecar career got under way.

Success with the Seeley-modified Matchless was immediate. During that first season, he earned his International licence, and in his first ever Isle of Man TT, finished in a splendid sixth position. By 1962 his performances were becoming more and more consistent, and, in fact, he became British Champion that year. Riding his sidecar outfit, he was the highest-placed British rider in the major international events. He took the British Championship again in 1964, and placed third in the World Championships, repeating the World place in 1966.

All this competitive motorcycling was in addition to running a business, which he began at a very early age. After leaving school, Colin had begun an engineering apprenticeship, but his dynamism soon led him to drop this, and shortly after he set up his own business, a retail motorcycle shop. He was just 18

Colin Seeley's interest in motorcycles stemmed from an early age. Here, at 14, he gets the feel of his father's Vincent.

Colin Seeley Racing

Sidecar racing was to prove a successful venture for Colin, shown here during the Dutch TT in 1964, the year he came third in the World Championship. The outfit is powered by a Rennsport BMW.

The MkI Seeley, with a Matchless G50 engine. The machine appeared in 1965 and was to set Colin on the road to becoming an independent manufacturer.

Motorcycle Road & Racing Chassis

The handmade MkI frame gave a new lease of life to both the Matchless G50 and AJS 7R engines.

years old at the time. Later, his dealership would become an AMC agent, which led to his close association with the AJS 7R and the Matchless G50.

Although it might appear that Colin Seeley had his plate full with running his business and a full sidecar racing programme, he still found time to build a solo racing frame. AMC ceased production of the 7R and G50 in the 1960s, but Colin felt that both engines still had something to offer, so he decided to build a frame to house the Matchless 500cc single. Many parts for the original machine were no longer available, and, in any case, Colin considered the original frames to be too heavy and complicated, so he set out to build his own.

He made it completely by hand, using a simple manual pipe bender to shape the frame tubes. These were made from 30mm diameter 16swg Reynolds 531 steel tubing, filled with silver sand during bending to prevent distortion. No jigs were used in the assembly. The whole frame was built on a metal-topped bench, working from a marked centre-line and with a threaded tool that could be adjusted to support the steering head at the required angles. The tubes were carefully fitted together and then welded by Colin, a self-taught welder. This MkI frame was fitted with a Matchless G50 engine and the first Seeley Racing solo motorcycle was born. The year was 1965.

At the start of the 1966 season, Derek Minter rode Seeley machines, and what a start it was. He won first time out on both a 350cc (7R) version and a 500cc (G50) model. A new era of frame building was on the way; at the time there were few independent frame makers to carry out this type of design and manufacture. That year also saw the AMC factory go into receivership, so Colin Seeley bought the whole racing department, that is the remainder of the spares and the rights to carry on production of the 7R and G50 engines. Included in the deal were the rights to the Manx Norton, which had previously been taken over by AMC. He continued to supply Manx spares from the residual stock, and manufactured some, such as cam followers, while there was a demand.

Colin (left) discusses the merits of the MkI Seeley with Derek Minter, who was to ride the machine on its successful debut, winning first time out.

as well as many notable battles with the Rickman Metisse – the culmination of the season saw Croxford winning the 1968 British Championship.

By this time, not only was the Seeley a very successful design, but the motorcycle fraternity had also taken to it, and its popularity continued to grow. In the meantime, Seeley continued to service existing AMC customers from the stock of original spares and parts manufactured by Colin Seeley Racing Developments Ltd.

All of this was a very bold step. Colin Seeley was about to undertake the manufacture of racing frames to house engines that had been dropped some years earlier by the original manufacturers. History, however, shows that the decision gave the racing motorcycle world new and competitive machines.

John Blanchard had taken over from Derek Minter as Seeley's rider during 1966, and continued into 1967. Success on the Seeley G50 was topped in that year when Blanchard took fourth place in the Isle of Man Senior TT. After this, however, a disagreement resulted in John Blanchard opting not to ride for Seeley, the talented John Cooper took over for the remainder of 1967.

In his usual quest to advance, Colin Seeley produced a MkII for the 1968 season. Although the MkI had proved both popular with its riders, and successful, Colin felt that it was too heavy. The new frame remained a full-loop type of very similar layout to the MkI, but the Reynolds 531 frame tubes were of smaller diameter at 28mm, while the tube wall thickness was reduced to 17swg. These changes resulted in a considerable cut in weight, without any reduction in structural performance.

Dave Croxford was to ride the new Seeley during the 1968 season, and again, the machine enjoyed many successes,

Colin proudly displays the MkII Seeley prototype during the Isle of Man TT in 1967; a MkI is in the background. The latest frame offered a considerable saving in weight without any loss of structural integrity.

Motorcycle Road & Racing Chassis

The MkIII Seeley displayed a complete change in frame layout. Diagonal tubes ran from the steering head down to the rear swinging arm pivot, the engine being suspended below them for improved accessibility.

The great Mike Hailwood demonstrates the Seeley MkI's potential.

Experience gained during a race season gives a designer the information required to ensure that his machine remains competitive, and Colin Seeley has always been a man to make the most of that experience. This was what led to the Seeley MkIII.

Colin refined the Seeley in 1970, producing the MkIV version. This is the works 636 version.

The MkIV continued in production until 1973: this 1972 version is typical of the breed.

Produced during 1969 and 1970, the MkIII still used the proven Reynolds 531 steel tubing for its frame, but the frame layout changed. It was no longer a full-loop type – there were no downtubes, and to produce the required structural performance,

Motorcycle Road & Racing Chassis

In 1967 a Seeley frame was built to house the URS four-cylinder 500, an engine originally developed by Helmut Fath for sidecar racing.

diagonal tubes ran from the steering head to the swingarm pivot. Colin had established that the fixing of these two points in relation to each other was a major factor in producing a stiff frame which, in turn, improved stability on the track or the road.

Another significant improvement was to engine access. The diagonal frame layout meant that the engine was suspended below the main tubes, leaving it exposed for work in situ, or making total removal much easier and quicker than with the full-loop MkI and MkII.

During 1969 Vincent Davey sponsored Mick Andrews, Dave Potter and Dave Croxford to ride Seeley 7R- and G50-engined machines, and a successful season for this sponsor was topped when Dave Croxford won the British 500cc Championship. The MkIII frame was an immediate success, showing that Colin Seeley Racing was continuing to develop frame technology to remain competitive on the track and in the commercial world.

The MkIII continued into 1970, but towards the end of that year, Seeley produced yet another frame advance, the MkIV. Although the MkIII had been successful, there was room for improvement, and on the MkIV, the long diagonal tubes ran up from the swingarm pivot to the bottom of the steering head, while the seat tubes were joined to the top of the steering head, the reverse of the previous arrangement. This resulted in a better

structural position for the main downtubes, and can be identified by the fact that these tubes are lower at the head end and, with AMC engines, run on each side of the engine rather than over it. Engine access was still excellent, and the MkIV frame was produced until Colin Seeley Racing ceased production of motorcycles in late 1973.

Throughout production of the Seeley frames, Colin made full use of the 7R and G50 singles, but these were far from being exclusive choices. Colin also designed and built many frames to house a wide range of engine makes and layouts. Some became series-production frames, produced in considerable numbers.

One of the first departures from the use of AMC engines occurred during 1967, when a frame was designed and built to house an in-line, four-cylinder 500cc URS engine. This had been developed originally by Helmut Fath and raced in sidecars. The performance of this engine had already been proven, having won Fath two world sidecar titles. Colin Seeley's frame did justice to the URS engine, the machine taking John Blanchard to a superb fourth place in the Ulster Grand Prix. Unfortunately, just after this important victory, Blanchard and Seeley parted company, so the potential of this rider and machine combination was never fully explored.

In 1969 Colin fitted the twin-cylinder Norton Commando

The across-the-frame engine layout of the URS can be clearly seen in this shot, as can the details of the Seeley frame.

power unit to a MkIII frame, on behalf of Norton dealer Kuhn Motors. Seeley supplied frame kits to Kuhn, which finished the build and sold the result as complete bikes. The Commando-engined Seeley was based on an existing frame, but in 1970 Colin designed and built a frame specifically to house the 500cc two-stroke QUB. This interesting project was a joint venture between Queens University, Belfast and Seeley. The engine was designed at the University, while Colin Seeley was not only involved in its manufacture, but also built the remainder of the bike. Although the result showed performance potential, it was troublesome, and the project died for a variety reasons before the problems could be overcome.

Another engine make to receive the Seeley treatment during this period was Husqvarna, the 500cc air-cooled twin. The same year also saw the introduction of the successful Yamsel prototype, ridden by John Cooper.

In the following year, Colin Seeley used his frame-making skills to house a variety of engine makes and types, and also built the first frames for Boyer Racing. One very significant point about 1971 was that a G50 engine and Seeley frame combination was

produced as a road bike. This road-going Seeley was named the Condor, a small production batch being completed and sold.

During 1970-1 Seeley was also contracted by the Italian Ducati factory to produce a series of race frames for its works 500cc V-twin. Paul Smart and Bruno Spaggiari were the riders, and two much-admired examples of these frames still reside in the UK. They were raced successfully with 750cc versions of the V-twin.

Another marked indication of the regard being shown for Colin Seeley's work came in 1971, when the legendary Barry Sheene, then a Suzuki works rider, suggested that Suzuki should consider a Seeley frame to replace the works frame of the XRO5, a 500cc, air-cooled two-stroke twin. The Suzuki riders were experiencing handling problems with this machine, hence the approach to Seeley. The resultant Seeley-framed version was ridden to an excellent third place in the 1971 Senior TT.

Barry Sheene then took this machine to Mallory Park and finished second to Giacomo Agostini on the 500cc MV Augusta, on which he had just won the Senior TT. In 1973 Sheene won both the British 500 Championship and the European 750

The MkIII frame provided the basis for the Kuhn Seeley Norton. Powered by the Norton Commando twin, the machine was assembled and sold by Kuhn Motors, using frame kits supplied by Seeley.

The remarkable Barry Sheene, in his early days, aboard a Kuhn Seeley Commando.

Alan Barnett and Colin Seeley with the QUB 500 at Brands Hatch during 1970.

Piloted by Alan Barnett, the QUB 500 is put through its paces at Brands. Sadly, the engine proved troublesome and development was halted.

John Cooper aboard the Yamsel prototype. Unlike QUB, this machine was successful.

In 1971 Seeley introduced the G50-engined Condor road bike, shown here being tested by motorcycle journalist Mick Woollett.

The great success during this period of the Seeley/Suzuki combination resulted in Colin receiving one of the newly-imported TR500 engines to use in another of his advanced projects during 1973. At the time, he was not only running Colin Seeley Racing Developments Ltd, but also overseeing the production of Brabham racing cars, which was in the transition from tubular space-frame chassis to monocoque construction. Seeing this development taking place in racing cars, he decided that motorcycles could also take advantage of this technology. Thus the Suzuki TR500 found its way into the first Seeley monocoque motorcycle.

Championship on a Suzuki-Seeley, now powered by a water-cooled, three-cylinder engine. This convinced Suzuki UK that Colin Seeley was the man to build its future chassis.

140

The Italian company Ducati recognized Seeley's skills when it commissioned Colin to build a series of frames for its 500cc V-twin. These were ridden by Paul Smart and Bruno Spaggiari.

The box-like monocoque construction was fabricated from aluminium sheet and riveted together. It had many advantages over a tubular steel frame construction. The sheet, being formed and riveted, did not suffer from the distortion problems common to welded frames, while the large-section box structure led to greater stiffness. Moreover, this type of construction offered ease of production.

The first example of the Seeley monocoque also utilized Colin Seeley's own custom-built magnesium alloy wheels and other specialized parts. At the time, it looked like the way forward for motorcycle chassis technology.

Although the machine was ridden with great promise by Barry Sheene, this interesting development came too close to the time when Colin Seeley Racing ceased trading. As a result, the potential of this very interesting project was never fulfilled.

Prior to the monocoque development, Colin Seeley was still busy building tubular frames for a variety of engines. In 1972 a Weslake 750cc parallel-twin was fitted to a Seeley frame, and the following year two big 750cc two-strokes – Kawasaki's air-cooled and Suzuki's water-cooled triples – were also tried.

Although 1973 had seen some interesting engines given the Seeley treatment, in most cases these were one-offs. With the 7R and G50 engines having reached the end of their competitive careers, and faced by the difficulties of maintaining a factory and a staff of almost 30 people in a declining market for racing or race-bred motorcycles, Colin Seeley ceased trading.

However, his skills and experience were not to rest too long, as in 1975 Seeley International was formed. Close contact with Honda UK resulted in the Seeley-Honda. comprising the Japanese company's SOHC, air-cooled four-cylinder engine in a Seeley frame.

It was such an impressive and successful machine that Honda UK contracted Colin Seeley to produce a batch of 150 road-going replicas of Phil Read's 1977 TT-winning machine. This was more of a conversion than a scratch-build and required the fitting of race-type fairings and ancillary equipment to an existing machine. So successful was this project that Honda soon engaged Seeley International on another contract.

Seeley had already built trials frames for Honda's TL200 four-stroke engine, which had been ridden by works riders,

Motorcycle Road & Racing Chassis

Colin Seeley's involvement with Brabham racing cars led to the development of a monocoque motorcycle frame. Powered by a Suzuki TR500 engine, it is shown here being tried for size by Ian Simpson, while Ron Carnell, competition manager for Duckham's, looks on.

and this resulted in a plan for Seeley International to produce 1000 production models. Unfortunately, after building just 300 TL200s, the company suffered considerable financial losses, so 1980 saw Seeley International cease trading as a motorcycle manufacturer in any form. However, Colin Seeley remained in business in other areas.

Original replicas

Although Colin Seeley's skill, flair and finesse are no longer being used in the design and construction of high-performance motorcycles, he has left his mark quite clearly in this area. In the 1960s and '70s, he built a wide range of machines for a wide range of engines, many of which were ridden with great success in competition. In fact, to this day, Seeley machines are still raced in classic events.

Throughout the period when Seeley machines were produced, they enjoyed a reputation for being well-built, very neat and having an excellent finish. The high standard of construction is borne out by the large number that are still in existence, and Seeleys are very much sought after by collectors and riders.

On the rare occasions that original examples come up for sale, they fetch high prices, sometimes even higher than those commanded by the factory-made machines using the same engines.

Although some Seeley machines were made in considerable

A variety of engines have found their way into Seeley frames over the years, including this 750cc Weslake parallel-twin.

The TL200 Honda-based trials bike proved a successful machine, but caused financial problems, leading to Seeley International being wound up.

The Seeley Honda was an impressive and successful machine. It led to further contracts from Honda to produce special machines.

The design of the Seeley Honda frame allowed removal of the cylinder head while the engine was still in the bike, something that was not possible on the standard machine.

numbers, the demand for these classics far outweighs the supply of genuine examples, which has resulted in replicas being produced. In fact, other frame makers have made a business of producing these copies. In most cases, they are marketed as replicas, and not sold as originals. Again, this emphasizes the respect and interest that motorcycling enthusiasts have for the machinery produced by Colin Seeley. It's a perfect example of imitation being the sincerest form of flattery.

fourteen

Segale

Italy has always been known as the home of powerful and beautiful automobiles. For many years, Luigi Segale has maintained that reputation in the world of motorcycling.

Luigi Segale entered the bike business as a conventional motorcycle dealer in 1972. However, within a comparatively short period of time, his talent for innovation and obvious engineering skills led to him carrying out conversions and modifications to production motorcycles, rendering them more suitable for competition in junior and national races.

The introduction of the FM1 programme in 1979 meant that, in addition to national racing, there were international classes for TT1-TT2 and endurance events, which produced a

This semi-monocoque, constructed from alloy honeycomb sandwich panels, is Segale's only departure from the use of steel tubing for motorcycle frames. The panels of the slab-sided structure were glued and riveted together to form a lightweight, yet very stiff chassis. The engine was a 750cc Ducati Desmo, its narrow layout making it ideal for this frame.

A Segale Honda 1000 endurance machine.

demand for suitable machines. This is
the point at which Luigi Segale began
the business for which he is now known
to the motorcycling world.

As with many constructors, Luigi
began by modifying production factory
frames to improve performance,
tailoring the modifications to suit each
customer's needs. It was inevitable
that eventually this would lead to the
manufacture of complete frames or
chassis for racing and sports use.
Demand resulted in a small, but
steady, production from this new
constructor.

The Segale Honda 1000 in action.

Segale

The Segale Honda 954.

and welder with whom he could collaborate on the construction of the new designs – Austrian Dirk Ilderbrand.

The collaboration worked extremely well, Segale designed bikes (including the bodywork), while Ilderbrand made the frames. However, in addition to a new range of successful racing and sports chassis, Luigi Segale also began to offer a comprehensive engine building and tuning service. This was made available to established racing teams as well as the inevitable stream of private riders. Also catered for were the riders of high performance sports machines who wanted to improve the power output of their engines still further.

Since Segale's business was a Honda agency, the principal engines to receive the Segale treatment came from that manufacturer. However, this was by no means an exclusive arrangement, as Kawasaki and Suzuki engines were also modified by Segale.

The frame construction of the 954. Note the use of the extended engine plates to carry both swingarm pivots and shock absorber mount.

Segale took a major step in 1980 by exhibiting his work at the Bologna Motor Show. This paid dividends and resulted in several frames being built to house Honda, Kawasaki and Suzuki engines. Versions of these machines were raced in F1 and F2 .

To capitalize on this new-found potential, and in an effort to turn out the best possible products, Luigi sought and found a top-class technician

In this photograph of the 954, the quality of construction is evident, particularly the tube bending and welding.

Motorcycle Road & Racing Chassis

During the Bologna Motor Show, the engineer Fabio Taglioni requested that Segale produce a special frame to house a 750cc Ducati Desmo engine. The A D Elle engine was chosen, and was particularly suitable for the project because it was very narrow. And it needed to be narrow, because of the special composite frame.

This was built from honeycomb sandwich panels. The complete load-bearing structure was assembled by gluing together the component parts with the assistance of some mechanical rivets. At the beginning of this project, problems were encountered in obtaining the aeronautical-type materials. However, with the co-operation of Signor Libanori of MV Agusta (who, as a matter of interest, was an MV rider in the 1950s and 1960s), and technical input from Signor Spairani, a director of SIAI MarcheTT1 (part of the Agusta aeronautical group), this one-off composite chassis was completed.

Until this excursion into the use of composites, Segale frames had almost all been manufactured from Cro-Mo steel tubing. In most cases, the engine would form a stressed member of the frame; that is, the front section of the frame would be attached to the front of the engine at the bottom end of the front downtube or tubes. Additional tubes would drop from the frame's top tube, or tubes, to the rear of the engine. These rear tubes would be attached to some plates, usually made from a material called Ergal 55. The plates formed attachments for the rear of the engine, and also the mounting and pivot for the rear suspension.

The rear swingarm design used on almost all Segale frames was unique. It was based on a magnesium casting, made in a clay mould and machined to the required specification as a final stage. The underside was of open section with diagonal bracing ribs cast in, and the combination of this open section and the use of magnesium provided a lightweight, but very strong, component.

From the beginning, Segale frames have incorporated another important feature, a series of eccentric rings and special bearings that carry the steering head and provide an adjustable front fork angle, which means that the wheelbase can be changed quickly and easily. This can be of major importance during a race meeting. The feature was not exclusive to race frames, but is available on all of Segale's frames, allowing discerning sports riders to full advantage of it.

The front forks used on Segale frames are also of Segale's own design and manufacture, and have been in production since 1979, when Marzocchi could no longer supply forks to Segale's requirements. They were designed and manufactured in collaboration with the well-known engineer Enrico Ceriani, who was responsible for specifying the materials used. The cast magnesium legs and yokes, or trapezes, were the work of Luigi Segale himself.

The front forks have proved very successful for both race and road use. In fact, they have proved so desirable that they were subsequently used, with various attachments, by the famous blue-blooded Bimota company.

Originally, the rear suspension of Segale's machines utilized American Fox adjustable shock absorbers, which were claimed to be well made and light in weight. However, Segale eventually introduced his own progressive rear suspension, which only used Ceriani double-action shock absorbers.

During the early years of frame manufacture, Segale fitted the marvellous Campagnolo cast five-spoke wheels especially for racing. Then, during 1981, the notable technician Roberto Marchesini left Campagnolo to work for Betor Spagnolo (maker of forks and shock absorbers), where he was given the task of producing racing type cast magnesium wheels to be marketed under the brand name of Betor.

At the Milan Motorcycle Show Marchesini offered the Betor wheels to Segale for Honda Italia's use in the world endurance championships and the Italian TT championship. In return for this generous offer, Segale gave Marchesini a design sketch of three-spoke cavity wheels, that is with hollow spokes.

Marchesini began producing these wheels in collaboration with the Marvic brand, and went on to offer them exclusively under the Marchesini label, and at one time all Segale bikes came with these wheels.

Up to and during 1980 Segale had produced many single or one-off machines, and to demonstrate the versatility of the designer, the models used many differing engine types, including the Ducati Desmo 750, Suzuki GSX550 and 750, Suzuki 1100R, Honda VF1000 and Honda CBX750.

After a very successful 1980 season, Luigi Segale received a proposal from Dr Alcidei, the commercial director of Honda Italia, that he should become involved in the sport side at national level, in the TT1 category at junior level and in some international endurance races. Segale produced four machines for Honda Italia, which supplied two semi-official engines with spares, the other two being supplied by Segale.

The following year, 1981, was a very positive one at the sporting level for Segale. Later that year, at the motorcycle show in Milan, he was to receive another important commission, this time from Dr Abbo, the Kawasaki importer. He wanted Segale to supply complete bikes less engines, which would be sold to private buyers who wished to compete in TT1 or TT2.

Two examples of these Segale Kawasakis were exhibited on Kawasaki's stand at the Milan Fair, and two were raced by Kawasaki Italia in the TT1 class that season. This Segale design

Segale

A Kawasaki-based Segale, examples being available for 900, 1000 and 1100cc engines.

An F1 endurance machine built around a Suzuki 750cc engine.

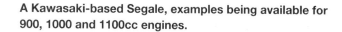

worked extremely well, the machine winning three Italian Championships: in 1982 and 1983 ridden by Roberto Suzzi, and in 1985 with Mauro Ricci. During 1984 Segale entrusted one of the Kawasaki machines to a German rider, Tedesco Gerschewer, who had great success with it. Two other Kawasakis went to Germany, being purchased by Serge Rosset of Annemasse. They then went to private riders.

Following the success of the machines supplied to Honda Italia, Dr Alcidei commissioned four more machines from Segale, again to utilize engines supplied on a semi-official basis. These machines were to compete in the national and international endurance championships as well as the Italian TT1 Championship.

To ensure that enough bikes and spares were available, Segale built eight machines, and these were a great success at national level, winning the TT1 Championship and the Endurance Championship. However, in the World Endurance Championship, they were denied success, recording only a sixth place in Germany and a seventh at Donington, England.

As well as the success enjoyed with Segale machines by the various importer teams, many private riders rode them to great effect. For example, during 1981, Segale supplied two French riders, Gherden and Ughen, with machines fitted with 1000cc Honda engines, and were used by the Frenchmen to seize second place in the Bol d'Or endurance race. They also achieved notable success in the World Endurance Championship as a private team. (Endurance racing has often proven to be a fine arena for privateers.)

For 1983 Honda Italia sold back to Segale

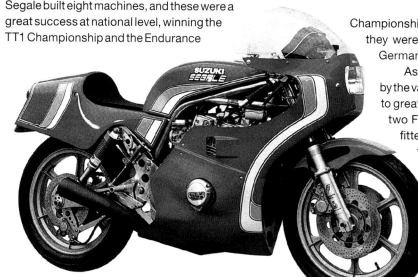

Another Segale Suzuki. This version can be supplied with a 750/1100cc GSX engine or the 1000cc TT1.

149

Mauro Rizzi in action in the Italian TT1 Championships, on the Segale 1000cc Honda.

the complete bikes, spares and tools originally supplied by him the season before. The price was attractive, but conditional on the bikes being raced at national level, and to make use of these machines, Segale engaged the riding services of Mauro Ricci, of Bologna, and Roberto Suzzi of Imola.

Although both riders were experts in their category, a rivalry seemed to grow between them, and part way through the season Suzzi left to ride for Luigi Termignoni. Amazingly, his machine in the new team was a Segale Kawasaki, so Segale was still very well represented. In fact Suzzi won the Italian TT1 Championship, while Ricci came third. So even with the loss of his team rider, Segale still won.

As well as successfully competing in the race series for big bikes – TT1, TT2 and endurance – Segale was successful in Italian 500 and 750 Championships. The first bikes used modified factory frames; a Kawasaki 500 and 750 in 1975, and a Honda 500 the following year. In '77, a Segale-modified works bike won the Italian National 500cc Championship, ridden by Gianni Del Carro.

Another successful season followed in 1978, with second place in the 500 Championship using a modified Honda ridden

by Angelo Laudati, and second place in the Italian 750cc Championship, with Marco Papa on a Kawasaki. Segale regained the 500 Championship the following year, and also the Italian Junior Championship – both titles secured by Angelo Laudati.

In the same year in which Laudati made his Championship double, Segale unveiled its Honda 954. This made its race debut in the five-hour International race at Zandvoort. Ridden by Laudati

The Supermono 650cc Segale Honda.

Although Luigi Segale has worked with machinery from several of the big manufacturers, 'Powered by Honda' has been the most prominent and successful signature on the fairing.

and Gianni De Carro, it came third, an amazing performance for a brand-new design. That year the bike also won the regional trophy with Angelo Laudati doing the riding. Segale won the regional trophy again in 1981 with a Honda 1000, the rider on this occasion being Walter Migliorati.

Segales won the Italian Endurance Championship of 1982 (ridden by Angelo Laudati and Arturo Venanzi) and came second and fourth in the 100-mile endurance race at Imola that year. In each case, the bikes were 1000cc Segale Hondas. In fact, it was a good year, as Robeno Suzzi won the Italian junior TT1 Championship on a 1000cc Segale Kawasaki.

Roberto Suzzi repeated that victory the following year while Mauro Rizzi (Segale Honda) was third. Segale missed the Championship win in '84 (Vittorio Scatola was second) but

rebounded to take the Italian Open Championship in 1985, thanks to Mauro Rizzi on a 1000cc Segale Kawasaki.

During that year the Segale business was transferred to its present site at 41 Galli Vigevano. At this point, Luigi Segale decided to give up his sporting activities to concentrate on the running of the dealership, and on producing some special machines to exhibit at the Milan Show. There were four of them, all based around the Honda VF1000 engine. No new machines appeared in 1986, but in 1987 Segale unveiled a new machine, using not a Honda, but a Suzuki engine, the 1100R. It was followed in 1989 by the first of the Supermonos, using Honda's 650cc single from the Dominator. This combination of punchy Honda four-stroke single and Segale chassis had wide appeal, with exports to Japan, England and Germany. Underlining his

Motorcycle Road & Racing Chassis

long-term commitment to Honda, the 1991 Milan Show saw Segale launch a machine based around the CBR600 RR. The intention was to offer motorcycling something exclusive, which it did quite effectively. This 650cc Honda engine and the Segale machine that housed it was to have wide appeal. It became a limited-production machine from the Segale workshops. The popularity of Segale's workmanship, coupled with this exciting design, had led to exports to Japan, England and Germany.

In 1991 Segale produced yet another new model for the Milan Show. On this occasion, it was the Segale Honda CBR 600RR, intended to offer the motorcycle world something exclusive, which it did quite effectively.

Segale continued on through the 1990s producing exciting machines for which he has become famous. The range as always was a mixture of competitive race machines and a selection of mouth-watering, distinctive, road going motorcycles. One such example was the Honda Fireblade SR900 of which Segale

produced a dozen customer examples. This was the last new model from Segale until the Honda-powered SVR1000R.

It was Luigi Segale's first new model for five years, and showed all the style and technical expertise the motorcycle world expected from the hand of this master craftsman. It was also the first production road machine from Segale to utilise a twin-cylinder engine, this being Honda's 996cc water-cooled V-twin. As on the Honda VTR it originally powered, the big twin was fuel injected with computer-controlled ignition. Power was transmitted via a six-speed gearbox, everything housed in a frame designed and built by Luigi himself. It could be altered to suit rider preference as well, with both steering head angle and seat height being adjustable. Twin floating discs at the front and a single disc at the rear took care of the stopping. Magnesium five-spoke wheels and alloy fuel tank, coupled with the use of carbon fibre and fibreglass bodywork helped to keep the dry weight down to a featherlight 175kg.

The beautiful Segale Honda SVR 1000R.

Another view of the Honda SVR 1000R-engined Segale.

Luigi Segale designed and built superb motorcycles in many forms for many years. No doubt about it, as an independent frame builder he made a huge contribution to the advancement of post-war motorcycle design.

1993 Segale SR 900, 1993.
(Courtesy Oli Tennent)

fifteen

Spondon Engineering

Spondon Engineering has been producing racing and road frames for nearly 40 years. The company was formed in 1969 by Bob Stevenson and Stuart Tuller, both of whom had ideal backgrounds for this sort of work. Bob Stevenson (now retired) had been an engineering apprentice with Rolls-Royce, receiving excellent training which gave him the basic skills that were to become invaluable in his hobby and, later, his business. That hobby was motorcycle racing, in which he took part for 14 years; he was still racing during the early days of Spondon Engineering. During his racing career, Bob rode a variety of machines, including a BSA Gold Star, a 7R AJS and a road racing 350cc Greeves. On this last machine, he was able to win a club championship.

The other half of the Spondon partnership, Stuart Tuller, had spent his apprenticeship as an electrician with British Rail.

An example of the Sparton, built as a joint venture between Spondon Engineering and Barton Motors. The chassis housed the three-cylinder engine built by the latter.

The Barton-built, 500cc four-cylinder engine that was used in later Spartons. This machine was used as the basis for the Silver Dream Racer of film fame.

This gave him a useful technical background, and like Bob, he raced bikes as a hobby. As is so often the case with independent frame makers, Bob and Stuart started out making modifications to their own bikes, which worked so well that other riders asked them to make similar changes to their machines. The demand grew steadily until it was clear that here was a viable business in the making – Spondon Engineering came into being.

In the main, work for the newly-formed business consisted of making modifications to existing racing machines. These were many and varied: different swingarms, where it was felt that an improvement could be made on the standard factory parts; frames were modified to accept different engines, or to change the positions of other components, or quite often to increase stiffness. In many cases, where modifications were of a structural nature, engineering design was called for to achieve the required structural performance. This design work was to prove invaluable in the coming years.

Although they concentrated on modification work, the partners already had experience of building complete frames. As early as 1964 they had designed and built a tubular steel frame to house a BSA Gold Star engine. This machine was unique in that the engine

Bob Stevenson mounted on a 350cc Greeves and competing at Skerries in Ireland in the late 1960s.

Motorcycle Road & Racing Chassis

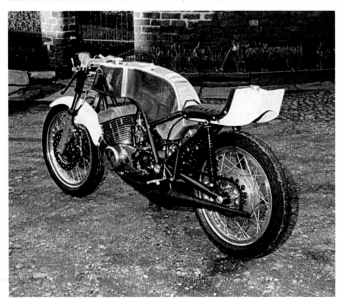

This 1973 Spondon chassis was built to house a 500cc twin-cylinder Suzuki engine.

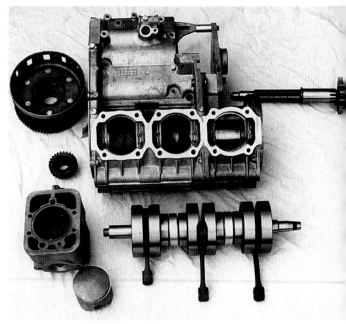

Karef Zegers' engineering skills are clearly demonstrated by these components. As can be seen, a new section has been grafted onto the crankcase of a twin-cylinder Yamaha TZ350, while a new crankshaft and extra cylinder barrel have also been added. The result was a powerful three-cylinder two-stroke.

was laid flat to lower the centre of gravity. The bold and innovative design demonstrated the potential of the partnership, particularly when it is realized – as with several innovators in this book – that the work was carried out in a garden shed.

The next venture into frame building was with a frame for a Honda 125. The completed machine was raced successfully by both Bob and Stuart, and this experience – both building the 125 frame and racing it – would prove invaluable. Spondon's first complete racing machine, built as a commercial venture, was a 125.

The first production machine was based on a tubular steel frame, designed to house an AS1 Yamaha engine. Although produced for road use, the engine proved both strong and tunable. In the Spondon frame, complete with the company's

The result of another joint venture, this time with engine builder Karef Zegers.

Spondon Engineering

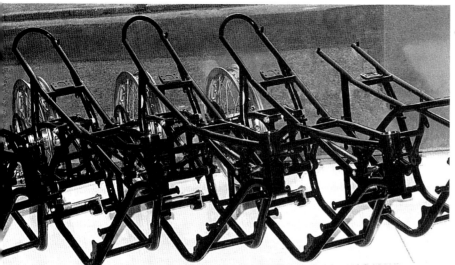

A 1978 production run of tubular steel frames for the Yamaha E-type engine.

own rear swingarm, it proved to be an affordable and very competitive package. So successful was it that over 120 examples were produced, which must be a record for a new company making only racing motorcycles.

The chassis design also proved good enough to accept a larger 350cc Yamaha engine and, once again, success on the

In 1980 Spondon began building this type of racer, based on a 250cc Rotax engine in a tubular steel frame.

Clive Horton on a 250cc Rotax-engined Spondon.

track led to more sales, though in this case it was something over 15 machines.

While the first production 125 was being produced, the usual one-offs and modifications, for which Spondon was renowned were still being carried out. However, during the early 1970s, a bold and adventurous project was to be undertaken, an alliance between Spondon Engineering and Barton Motors, with the aim of producing a complete 500cc racer.

The new machine was to be called the Sparton, a package that would be offered for sale by both companies involved. The unique aspect of this project was that Barton Motors was to produce the engine, while Spondon Engineering would design and build the rolling chassis, and assemble the complete machine.

The engine for the Sparton was a hybrid, consisting of a 380cc Suzuki crankcase to which were fitted specially-designed barrels, the result being a three-cylinder 500. It was housed in a Spondon tubular steel frame and swingarm, and the result was a competitive racer. Bob Stevenson raced a Sparton successfully himself. This attracted the attention of clubman racers.

The Sparton was developed further when it received a completely new engine layout. Although the 500cc capacity was retained, this later engine was of a square-four configuration. Again, it was built by Barton Motors, and over the next few seasons, between other work, the two companies built and sold 26 examples.

The early 1970s saw Spondon involved in another collaboration, which produced another 500 with a hybrid engine. The latter was a clever conversion by Karef Zegers, being based on the crankcase of the Yamaha TZ 350cc twin-cylinder two-stroke. Another section of crankcase was grafted on, extending it to accept a third cylinder. Suitable cylinders were prepared and fitted, and a new crankshaft to suit. The result was a race-reliable, 500cc three-cylinder two-stroke.

Bolted into a Spondon tubular steel chassis, the bike was intended as an over-the-counter racer, and in this very competitive area attracted enough attention from club racers for twelve to be sold.

From the mid-1970s up to 1980, Spondon was very busy in the production of replica frames, centred on the E-type Yamaha engines of 250 and 350cc. The E-type had Yamaha's first mass-produced monoshock chassis, and the tubular steel replica offered by Spondon proved so good that, over a few

A 1982 Spondon chassis with a 500cc four-cylinder engine. Note that although this is a tubular frame, the tubing is of square section and is aluminium. This proved a significant step for the company in the design and construction of motorcycle frames.

the popularity of racing machines with larger capacity engines was growing, and Spondon was able to take advantage of this by producing replica chassis to house the Yamaha TZ750 power unit. As the '70s gave way to the 1980s, Spondon was still producing replica chassis for the 350cc Yamaha engine, but had incorporated a major change. Although a replica in layout, the Spondon frame was now built from 2.5cm square-section alloy tubing. This move produced a chassis that gave the required structural performance, but showed a considerable weight saving over the tubular steel version.

The use of alloy tube as a chassis material proved popular and successful. At first, these frames were only built for the 350cc engines, but later 250cc versions were also made, one winning the 1982 British 250cc Grand Prix. In just two seasons, 30 of these alloy tube chassis were sold.

Successful it might be, but Spondon didn't stand still, and the next development was the use of larger section tubes in extruded form, of commercial-grade alloy. Among the machines

Built during the early 1980s, this frame utilized steel tubing to house the four-cylinder Suzuki engine. The jig-welded method of construction is evident.

short seasons, 113 examples were produced. This work was interspersed with the production of one-off chassis and, of course, many modifications.

The replica chassis produced by Spondon Engineering were very strong, and also gave the machines excellent handling. As a result, the company's reputation grew, bringing in much more business. The building of replica frames continued to be good business for Spondon with the production of a steel chassis to house the FG-type Yamaha engine. Again, engine capacities were 250 and 350cc. The popularity of this replica chassis was wide, and continued into the early '80s, with 135 frames produced.

Towards the end of the 1970s,

The Spondon twin-spar frame, constructed from extruded-alloy sections. In this case, the engine is a single-cylinder Rotax 500. The machine was built to race in the popular European Formula Single.

to gain an advantage from the extruded alloy sections were some built for Dr Joe Erlich, of EMC fame. These were fitted with Rotax 250cc units. Although Spondon had built frames for EMC using the 2.5cm square-section tubing, the later versions took full advantage of the improvements offered by the extrusions and proved particularly successful. Spondon would supply 35 machines for Dr Erlich to race under the EMC banner.

Having seen the great advantages offered by the extruded alloy sections, both in ease of manufacture and the all-important improvements to structural performance, Spondon took this theme further: by the mid-1980s, it had optimized the use of alloy by the use of special extruded sections of its own design. It had financed the dies for the extrusions, ensuring that those designs remained exclusive to Spondon.

In the main, three extrusions were used, all rectangular in shape, but of different sizes. One aspect of the largest extrusion was that one corner was flattened, and this part was used for the main members of backbone or twin-spar frames, the flattened corner being positioned at the top, which gave the chassis a rounded-off appearance.

From a structural point of view, the larger sections of the extrusions automatically improved the bending stiffness and torsional performance of the frame members, but these qualities were further enhanced by integral longitudinal spars, or webs, inside the extrusions. In the largest section, two webs produced a cross-section that had the appearance of three square tubes joined together; the smaller extrusions each had a single web. The webs stabilized the outer walls when bending loads were applied to the extrusions, resisting any buckling. As a result, a far greater bending load was required to force the extrusion walls to buckle.

So, without changing the outside dimensions of the extrusion, its stiffness was greatly improved. The overall performance and quality of these extrusions were further

A complete Spondon racer, powered by a 250cc Rotax. Note the use of square-section alloy tubing. This type of construction was in use during 1983-84.

By 1988 Spondon was using alloy extrusions as a standard chassis material, as this four-cylinder Kawasaki example shows.

Spondon Engineering

This 1991 Spondon frame shows the use of a wider range of extrusion sizes. It also demonstrates the excellent overall design and finish that has come to be expected from the company's road bikes.

enhanced by the use of higher-grade 7020 alloy.

The use of these specialized extrusions has since become Spondon's standard method of frame construction. Backbone or twin-spar chassis would have the largest extrusion as the backbone or spars, while the smaller-section extrusions, would form the remainder: engine mounts, subframe for the seat, etc. Another advantage of using this variety of extrusions was that Spondon was able to use them in another structural application, the highly stressed rear swingarm.

Extrusions lend themselves to being bent and welded, and because of the latter, more than one size or type of extrusion can be used in the same structure. In addition, load-bearing points – engine mounts, chain adjusters, etc. – are all easily incorporated, making this type of construction very versatile from both the structural and production aspects.

During the 1980s, Spondon was to widen its horizons and enter new markets. In the beginning, it had used its experience and expertise to produce a very wide range of racing machines,

In 1991 Spondon was still producing replica chassis, as this 250cc Yamaha B racer shows.

This frame was designed to cope with a high-performance powerplant, intended for a road bike based on a turbocharged, four-cylinder Suzuki engine.

Motorcycle Road & Racing Chassis

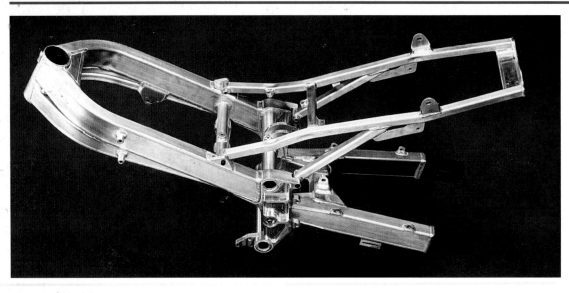

but this new era was to see it beginning to design and manufacture road bikes.

Spondon was able to offer the road bike customer a special service, tailoring the whole machine to meet specific requirements. This included the choice of engine, which could be of almost any make or type, and as time went by, the company would develop road bikes around most of the popular suitable engines.

The road bike business became a significant part of Spondon Engineering's production, and to enhance this aspect, it began to build road bikes of its own design, based on popular power units. Although road bikes were a major business for Spondon during the '80s, it still produced a considerable number of racing machines. The company's

A good example of Spondon's frame work. This design utilizes several different sizes of alloy extrusion, as well as machined sections to connect the lower ends of the twin spars to the rear swingarm pivot. A Yamaha 750cc twin completes this racing machine.

Where it all started – the production of racing machines. Brian Reid is shown mounted on a Spondon-built 350cc Yamaha, just one of many.

output of complete machines was made up of approximately 75 per cent road bikes and 25 per cent racing bikes.

During 1990, Spondon was contracted by Norton to produce the chassis for the new F1 road bike. This was of the twin-spar type and made full use of alloy extrusions, and was designed to house Norton's liquid-cooled rotary engine.

Spondon supplied the complete chassis, which included the rear swingarm and subframe, while Norton completed the assembly. This was a significant step for Spondon, as it had to produce 200 complete chassis to meet the homologation requirements so that the machine could be classified as a production bike for racing purposes.

Motorcycle Road & Racing Chassis

The Spondon-framed Yamaha TDM 850 twin, first built during late 1989.

continued to service the motorcycle world by the supply of parts, many made in-house, and the supply of replacement frames for almost any motorcycle.

By 1995 Spondon had another design in production, this one taking the popular Honda FireBlade engine. It did well for Spondon too, and, while its production volumes weren't quite up to those of Honda, 25 machines was a respectable batch, many of them exported, including three to Moscow. Two years later, the company reverted to its old-style cantilver rear suspension system for a frame to take the Honda CBX six-cylinder engine, because Bob Stevenson felt that the cantilever still worked

As well as fulfilling the Norton contract, Spondon Engineering also designed and built a series of machines for a Far Eastern customer, and while these production runs were being carried out, the one-offs and specials carried on, as they always had.

At the beginning of 1992 Spondon produced a unique frame to house the Harley Davidson 883 Sportster engine. The swingarm pivot was on the gearbox centre line, and the rear shock was mounted horizontally, on the left-hand side of the engine. The Spondon Harley was well received, and the company built eighteen of them. Later that year it built a retro Kawasaki Z1000 frame to take standard bodywork. The frame itself was fabricated from alloy tube and incorporated modern wheels and tyres. Ten were built for customers from South Africa, Japan and the USA.

Between the various designs brought out by Spondon, the company

Early in 1992 Spondon produced the machine shown here, with Harley-Davidson's 883 Sportster engine.

A late 1992 product from Spondon shows the retro Kawasaki Z1000.

better than anything else, and other later Spondon frames used the cantilver system as well. Seven of those CBX frames were built, but only one of a 1999 model to suit the Yamaha TDM850, and a later design for the Harley-Davidson 1450cc V-twin. A similar fate befell the alloy frame built the same year for the Honda CBR1100 Blackbird power unit – only three of those were sold. And the Spondon frame for Suzuki's TL1000 (again, only three sold) which had a complicated rear suspension arrangement due to he lack of space and exhaust layout around the big V-twin.

In 2000, a frame for the Suzuki GSX-R1300 Hayabusa was more successful – ten were built, most going to Germany. By this time, the Yamaha R1 was the class-leading sports bike, and late in 2001 Spondon began to produce a chassis to suit it, offered with either a gull swingarm or single-sided swing arm. Of all the chassis that Bob Stevenson has cast his magic over, this is one of his favourites.

Another Spondon design that is in current build is a chassis for the Suzuki GSX-R1000. With this excellent engine as a base, this chassis has been a popular one, and at the time of writing ten have been sold.

One very interesting alternative from Spondon is an alloy frame for the original Suzuki Bandit. Designed to take all standard factory parts including bodywork, swingarm, rear suspension, the amazing thing about this frame is that it is a staggering 17 kilos lighter than

The early 1997 design from Spondon shown here uses the Honda CBX 1000 engine.

Motorcycle Road & Racing Chassis

the standard unit. In fact, Suzuki is a good source of business for Spondon, and its original GSX-R frame, dating from 1991, remains the most successful to date, with over 100 supplied to customers all over the world.

On top of all its other work Spondon will still undertake the design and build of one-off machines if requested, for road or race use, as well as considerable work coming from the manufacture of steel chassis or frame replacements for many of the old favourites, such as Norton, Molnar Moux, Seeley, Drixton, Aermacchi, Egli Vincent and the Ducati 250. What with this, its own quick-release rear wheel system for Superbike racers, and production of its own brake callipers, discs, swingarms and many other parts, it looks like Spondon will be kept busy for a long while yet.

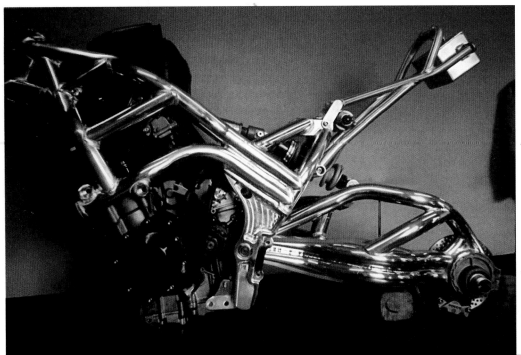

During 2001 Spondon produced this Yamaha R1-based bike.

A late 1999 design from Spondon housing the Suzuki TL1000 V-twin.

Spondon Engineering

Another design from Spondon late in 1999 was a frame to take the Honda CBR1100 Blackbird engine, shown here.

At the beginning of 2000 Spondon was producing this Suzuki GSX-R1300 powered machine.

During 2001 production began on the Spondon design to house the Yamaha R1. This model is still being produced.

Another model designed and built during 2001 was a frame for the Harley-Davidson big twin.

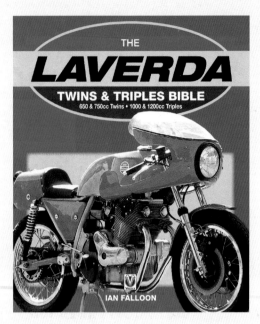

Laverda Twins & Triples 1968-1986 Bible
by Ian Falloon

£29.99* • ISBN: 978-1-845840-58-7

The large capacity Laverda twins and triples were some of the most charismatic and exciting motorcycles produced in a golden era. With a successful endurance racing programme publicizing them, Laverda's twins soon earned a reputation for durability. Here is the year-by-year, model-by-model, change-by-change record.

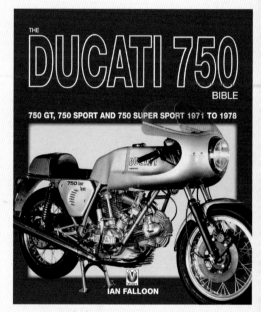

The Ducati 750 Bible
by Ian Falloon

£29.99* • ISBN: 978-1-845840-12-9

When the great Ducati engineer Fabio Taglioni designed the 750 Ducati in 1970, there was no way he could have known how important this model would be. The 750, the Formula 750 racer and the Super Sport became legends: this book celebrates those machines.

The Moto Guzzi Sport & Le Mans Bible
by Ian Falloon

£29.99* • ISBN: 978-1-845840-64-8

Lino Tonti managed to take the large V7 Moto Guzzi touring engine and create a spectacular sporting motorcycle, the V7 Sport, in 1971. This remarkable machine evolved into the stylistic 850 Le Mans, another landmark Italian motorcycle. Here is a year-by-year account of development and specification changes of a great series of motorcycles.

"Guzzi fans will appreciate this history of the Tonti-frame twins made between 1971 and 1993. Design is big and bold, with some great period pics, and it's well researched." *Octane*

Edward Turner – The man behind the motorcycles
by Jeff Clew

£17.99* • ISBN: 978-1-845840-65-5

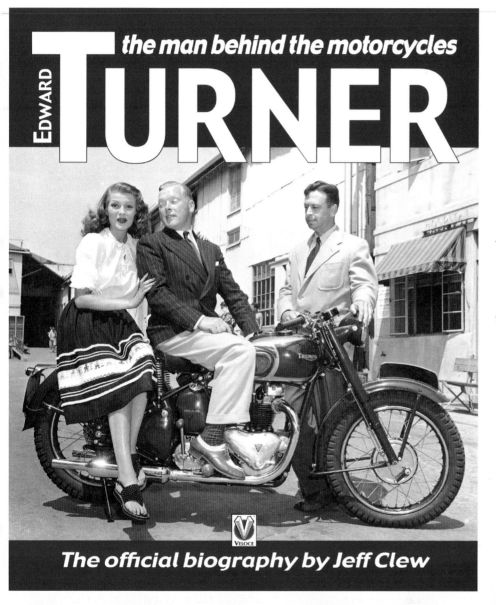

the man behind the motorcycles

EDWARD TURNER

VELOCE

The official biography by Jeff Clew

For the first time the life of Edward Turner, one of Britain's most talented motorcycle designers, is revealed in full, so this is much more than just another book about Triumph motorcycles. Although seen by many as an irascible man who ran a very tight ship, it is an inescapable fact that that his was a highly profitable company. Turner's hugely successful sales campaign after World War 2 stunned America's own manufacturers and had long-lasting repercussions on their own home market. As Bert Hopwood once said to the author, Turner was an inventive genius who had the flair for pleasing shapes and an uncanny ability to perceive what the buying public would readily accept, and produce it at the right price. No one will deny the impact made at the annual Motor Cycle Show by his Ariel Square Four in 1931, his superbly-styled single cylinder Tiger models in 1936, and his revolutionary Speed Twin that dominated the show in 1937. Even better was to follow with his post-war Thunderbird and Bonneville twins.

"It is full of intriguing detail of his work and his life, and makes for a very interesting and enjoyable read." Vintagebike.co.uk

"Long overdue, this deeply researched work by Jeff Clew gets past Turner's irascible exterior to reveal the man, his life and work, and the huge contribution to his country and the evolution of the motorcycle. Featured are many images from the Turner family private photograph collection. This book is an excellent addition to any enthusiast's library." *The Visitor Magazine*

*prices subject to change. P&P extra. Visit www.veloce.co.uk or call 01305 260068 for details.

The Triumph Trophy & Tiger Bible
by Harry Woolridge

£30.00* • ISBN: 9-781-904788-02-7

The complete year-by-year history of the Trophy (and unit construction Tiger) twins from 1949 to 1983. Includes original factory model photos, technical specifications, colour schemes, engine and frame numbers, model type identification, and details of Trophy and Tiger achievements. The complete source book.

The Triumph Tiger Cub Bible
by Mike Estall

£35.00* • ISBN: 978-1-904788-09-6

The full history of the popular Triumph Cub motorcycle. This ultimate reference source book covers every aspect of these machines, including 22 detailed model profiles, delivery details, technical design specifications, military, police and competition bikes, plus the full story behind the model's production run.

Index

Abbo DR 148
AEI 91
Aermacchi 28, 128, 166
Agostini 10, 30, 82,137
AJS 33, 49, 73, 131, 154
Albion St Motors 105
Alcidei DR 148, 149
AMC 132, 133, 136
America 124
Anelli, Luigi 28
AP 61
Arabic 72
Astralite 111
Australia 83, 124
Avon & Somerset Police 117

Bakker, Nico 9-11, 13, 17, 129
Ballington, Kork 10, 51
Barcelona 33, 106
Barry, Des 59
Barton Motors 158
Bayford, Steve 51, 65
Betor 48, 148
Bianchi 23
Bimoto 23-26, 28, 30, 31, 148
Blanchard, John 133
BMW 11, 17, 33, 43, 83, 91, 105, 116, 117
Bol d'Or 106, 149
Bologna 147, 148, 150
Boyce Racing 137
Brabham Racing Cars 140
Brands Hatch 106
Brembow 11, 13
British GP 93
British National Championship 60, 66, 128
British Rail 73, 154
BSA 33, 40, 49, 120, 125, 154, 155
Burnett, Roger 99
Burroughs, Eddie 122
Butaco 125, 126, 129

Cagiva 11
Camfield, Tiny 120
Campagnolo 148
Cariani, Enrico 148
Cathcart, Alan 110
Cecotto 10, 31
Ceriani 48, 111
Chevron Cars 91
Chittenden, Derek 72, 76, 78
Colin Seeley Racing Developments 133
Cooper, John 133, 137
Cornu, Jacques 45
Cosworth 44, 91
Cowie, John 105
Cresent 51
Croxford, Dave 133, 136
CZ 91

Davenport, Phil 111
Davey, Vincent 136
Decorite 54
Degens, Dave 32, 40, 41
Del Carro, Gianni 150, 151
Dixon, Darren 54
Donington 149
Dresda Autos 32, 33, 37-41, 101, 104
Ducati 20, 30, 43, 73, 93, 137, 148, 166
Dugdales 93
Duke, Jeff 41
Dumfries, Jonny 114
Dunlop 106
Dunlop, Joey 99

Earls Court 117
Egli Fritz 42-48, 166
Ekerold 31
EMC 55
Emmelt, Sean 64, 66
England 124, 149, 152
England, Ivor 124
English 33
Erlich, Dr J 55
Evemy, Herbert 125

Falappa 31
Fath, Helmut 128, 136
Ferrari 31
Fox 148
France 48
Frane, Alistair 105

Gardener, Wayne 99
George, Alex 106
German 45
Gerschewer Tedesco 149
Gherden 149
Gilberts of Catford 106
Gilera 81
Girling 48, 105
Godet, Patrick 48
Godfrey, Phil 111
Goldsmith, Andy 52
Gould, Rodney 33
Grand Prix World Championship 66
Grant, Mick 5, 51, 52, 99
Greeves 154
Grimeca 48

Hailwood 82, 105
Harley-Davidson 41, 43, 164, 165
Harris, Lester 49, 51
Harris Performance Products 49, 50, 52, 53,
    55, 61, 63, 65, 110, 129
Harris, Steve 49, 51
Hartog, Will 10
Haslam, Ron 99, 105, 106
Hawkstone 124

Haydon, James 66
Hejira 72
Hejira Racing HRD Ltd 74, 78, 79
Herron, Tom 93, 105
Heuwen, Keith 60
Hickman, Dave 93
Hodgson, Neil 66
Honda 10, 11, 17, 20, 28, 30, 37, 40, 43, 45,
    48, 54, 75, 82, 83, 94-96, 99, 104-106, 112,
    118, 128, 141, 147-152, 154, 165
Hossack, Norman 116
Husqvarna 129, 137

Ikuzawa, Tetsu 59
Indian 46, 48
Irons, Kenny 60
Isle of Man 55, 93, 94, 130
Italian 31, 148
Italy 45, 145
Ivey, Bill 128

Jansen, Nic 124
JAP 41
Japan 59, 94, 152, 164
Japanese 30, 43, 48, 92, 94, 141
John Player Norton 99

Katayama, Takasumi 94, 99
Kawasaki 10, 11, 28, 38, 43-45, 48, 52, 53,
    56, 60, 75, 105, 108-110, 112, 114, 116,
    118, 128, 147, 148, 150, 151, 164
Kawasaki Motors UK 68
Kidd, Eddy 114
Koni 47, 48, 99
Konig 51
Kuhn Motors 136
Kultalahti Vesa 59

Lancashire Police 117
Laudati Angelo 150, 151
Lavado 31
Laverda 43
Le Mans 106
Leaman, Ken 117
Libanori, Signor 148
Llderbrand, Dirk 147
Lockheed 48, 111
Lucchinelli 31
Lunde, Martin 52
Lundin, Sten 124

Machin, Steve 93
MacMillan, Denis 105
Magni 81, 83-88
Magni Arturo 81, 82
Maico 129
Malaysian 68
Mallory Park 128, 137
Mamola, Randy 52

Manley, Steve 54
Manx 93
Marchesini 61
Marchesini, Roberto 148
Marshall, Roger 91, 99, 106, 107
Marvic 148
Marzocchi 48, 111, 148
Matchless 122, 128, 130-132
Maxton Engineering 91-96, 99
McGregor, Graham 59, 107
McNab 106
McNab, Peter 101
McQueen, Steve 124
Mellor, Phil 54, 61
Mertens 31
Metisse 120, 121, 124, 125, 129, 133
Middelburgh, Jack 10
Mikuni 44
Milan 148, 151, 152
Minter, Derek 133
Mitchenal, Doug 121
Mocheck 105
Molnar 166
Montesa 120
Moody, Jim 66
Morbidelli 10, 28
Morton, Chris 93
Moto Guzzi 85, 89, 90, 118
Motor Cycle Weekly 118
Motor Racing Enterprises 113
Moux 166
Moyse, Asa 58, 60, 105, 109
Murray, Bernard 93
MV Agusta 81, 82, 85, 86, 137, 148
MZ 48

Nardo 45
Nation, Trevor 52, 54, 59
New Milton 120, 125
Newbold, John 51, 52
Newell, Malcolm 117, 118
Nichols, Roger 105
North, Rob 102
Norton 32, 33, 42, 128, 132, 136, 163, 164,
    166
Noyce, Graham 129
NSU 41
Nürburgring 45, 106

Ohlins 61
Osborne Tony 105
Oxley Matt 59

P&M 107, 108, 111, 112
Paget, Clive 59
Pagets 61
Papa, Marco 150
Paris 37
Parrish, Steve 51, 52, 59, 60, 93
PDQ 113, 114
Peckett, Richard 101, 104-106, 111, 112

Phillips, Mark 56, 61
Piaggio 119
Pileri 31
Porsche 40
Powell, Max 76
Probe 117

Quaife RJ Engineering 112
Quasar 117
Quasar Motor Cycles Ltd 117
Queens University Belfast 137

Rawlings, Dave 66
Read, Phil 10, 31, 52
Reliant 117, 118
Reynolds 37, 53, 121, 132, 133, 135
Ricci, Mauro 149, 150
Rickman 120, 121, 126, 133
Rickman, Derek 120
Rickman, Don 120
Rieju 48
Rizzi, Mauro 151
Roberts, Eddie 93
Rolls-Royce 154
Rosset, Serge 149
Rotax 11, 54, 60, 75
Rothmans International 99
Royal Enfield 46-48, 129
Rumi 33
Rutter, Tony 93, 106
Rymer, Terry 64

Sachs 48, 75
Sarron, Christian 33
Sauber Petronas Engineering AG 68
Scaillet, Hubert 122
Scarab 48
Scarborough 37
Scatola, Vittorio 151
Scott, Richard 99
Seeley 49, 132, 133, 136, 137, 141, 166
Seeley, Colin 130, 134, 140, 144
Seeley International 141, 142
Segale, Luigi 145-148, 150-153
Sheene, Barry 33, 51, 54, 65, 137, 141
Shell 64
Shell Harris Team 66
Sherco 48
Shule 45
Siai Marchetti 148
Siff Bronze Co 122
Smart, Paul 137
Smit Cees 13
Snetterton 37, 104, 112
South Africa 52, 164
Spa 104
Spaggiari, Bruno 137
Spagnolo Betor 148
Spairani, Signor 148
Spondon Engineering 111, 154-156, 158-161,
    163-166

Sprayson, Ken 121
Stevenson, Bob 154, 165
Storey, Ron 59
Stroud, Andrew 64
Surtees 82
Suzuka 59
Suzuki 10, 11, 20, 28, 30, 40, 43, 44, 49, 50,
    52, 53, 60, 68, 75, 86, 92, 94, 105, 109, 112,
    116, 118, 128, 137, 140, 141, 145, 148, 151,
    158, 165
Suzzi, Roberto 149-151
Swan, Ray 59, 110
Swiss 47
Switzerland 48

Taglioni, Fabio 148
Tamburini, Massimo 23
Tate, Bob 117, 118
Tate, Percy 37
Termignoni, Luigi 150
Toleman, Bernie 105
Trimby, Mike 52
Triumph 37, 43, 49, 51, 102, 111, 120, 122, 124,
    125, 128
Tuller, Stuart 154

URS 136
Ughen 149
Ulster GP 136
USA 164

Vilaseca, Christian 37
Villa 31
Vincent 42, 43, 48
Vuccini 31

Walker, Clint 124
WCM 68
Webb, Larry 113, 116
Weber, Marelli 90
Wells, Jim 56, 105, 108, 109
Westlake 141
White Power 11
William, Charlie 93, 94
William, John 93
Williams, Ron 91-94, 96, 99
Wilson & Sons 117
Wood, Stan 93
World Championship 56, 59, 60
World Endurance Championship 149

Yamaha 10, 11, 17, 28, 30, 33, 40, 48, 51, 54,
    59-61, 64, 66, 75, 93, 94, 96, 116, 118, 154,
    155, 158, 159, 165

Zandvoort 150
Zeger, Karef 158
Zundapp 128, 129

Tales of Triumph Motorcycles & the Meriden Factory

by Hughie Hancox

£19.99* • ISBN: 978-1-901295-67-2

A delightful and often humorous account of life with the Triumph motorcycle company in its hayday. Hughie tells the story of his time in the famous Meriden factory and of his many adventures with Triumph motorcycles and Triumph people and, by so doing, records the fascinating inside story of one of Britain's greatest motorcycle marques.

"You will enjoy every page." *Old Bike*
"Pushing for the best book of the year title."
Motorcycle Sport & Leisure

Triumph Speed Twin & Thunderbird Bible

by Harry Woolridge

£25.00* • ISBN: 978-1-904788-26-3

The definitive history of Triumph's two most popular models in the 1940s and 1950s. In-depth information on the Thunderbird not previously available. Year-on-year development history on both models. Year-by-year engine and frame numbering enabling correct identification. Colour schemes used throughout the model life. Photographs and colour prints showing each model in detail. Competition success and achievements for both models.

British 250cc Motorcycles 1946 to 1959: an era of ingenious innovation

by Chris Pereira

£15.99* • ISBN: 978-1-904788-12-6

From 1946 up to 1959, the 250cc motorcycle class in Britain was supported almost entirely by privately built Specials and Hybrids. This book recalls the men and machines involved, and traces their history and development, in what was clearly the most technically innovative class of Road Racing in the 1950s.

Jim Redman M.B.E. – Six times World Motorcycling Champion

by Jim Redman

£14.99* • ISBN: 978-1-901295-35-1

Reprinted by popular demand! This is the autobiography of a motorcycle racing legend. Jim Redman won World Championships six times in the 250cc and 350cc classes during the 'Golden Era' of motorcycle racing. Over 100 illustrations support this extraordinary life story.

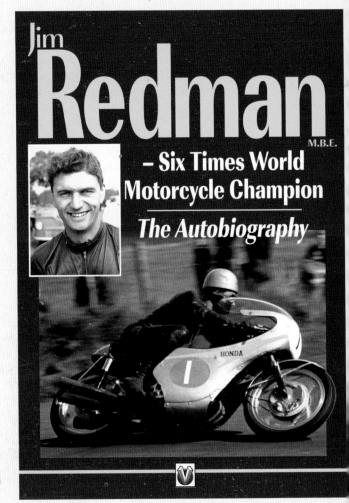